Improv Ideas

A book of games and lists

Compiled, Created and Invented by
Justine Jones and Mary Ann Kelley

MERIWETHER PUBLISHING LTD.
Colorado Springs, Colorado

Meriwether Publishing Ltd., Publisher
PO Box 7710
Colorado Springs, CO 80933-7710

www.meriwether.com

Editor: Art Zapel
Assistant editor: Audrey Scheck
Interior design: Jan Melvin

Library of Congress Cataloging-in-Publication Data

Kelley, Mary Ann, 1948-
    Improv ideas : a book of games and lists / by Mary Ann Kelley and Justine Jones.
        p. cm.
    Includes bibliographical references and index.
    ISBN 978-1-56608-113-9 (pbk.)
1. Improvisation (Acting) 2. Games. I Jones, Justine, 1948- II. Title
    PN2071.I5K45 2006
    792.02'8--dc22

                    20050300875

            4   5   6   12   13   14

Dedication

To Our Muses

Darryl and Nick

Chris and Charles

And to all those students who, throughout the years,

played through these games and learned without knowing it.

They did the real work.

Contents

Games and Lists

About This Book

And Now Some Answers

Using the ever-popular question and answer format, Justine and Mary Ann answer questions that may have never occurred to you.

Why a whole book of games and lists?

After teaching for a combined sixty-two years, we have become familiar with most of the texts on teaching drama and theatre, especially the texts on theatre and drama games. Since most people who teach drama have not been lucky enough to observe a master teacher using improv as a teaching tool, most of us have developed our teaching strategies through trial and error, adapting Spolin or Johnstone to our various groups. We found ourselves reading through a shelf full of books and picking and choosing what we hoped would work that day to illustrate the concept we wished to teach. Finally, we became frustrated with carrying around five or ten books, each with one or two useful ideas, not to mention the stacks of papers and sticky notes with our own ideas. We tired of long descriptions that were not to the point. We complained to each other and anyone who would listen about our plight and longed for a simple-to-use game source, perhaps accompanied by lists of ideas for those days when we didn't have time or creativity to think up new options. That was the birth of the first version of this book!

Many teachers and group leaders feel that spontaneity is best learned by *just doing it!* Some of us have found that having fast-paced group sessions with very few pauses serves this goal best. However, even experienced leaders sometimes run short of ideas or draw blanks after particularly long sessions or busy days. Hence, this book of lists which can serve as memory jogs or completely new inspirations. Be aware, of course, that generating ideas from the group is always best. Try using the games with beginning groups as icebreakers while supporting the group's own ideas.

Asking groups to list ideas that will be used the next session often lends anticipation for the next activity as well as providing wonderful lists.

Participants really enjoy picking their ideas at random — somewhat like a fortune cookie — from an interesting container. For this reason we have included a CD-ROM so you may print these lists directly onto heavy paper or onto labels to stick onto index cards. See *You've Gotta Have a Gimmick!* in Appendix 3, for list-handling ideas.

Note: When letting participants (especially students) write their own ideas to draw from a hat, be sure to check them before letting others draw. We have learned this the hard way.

Improv Ideas is arranged with the lists in alphabetical order to make it easier for you to find lists to use with your own games.

What do you mean by improvisation?

When we talk about improvisation, or improv, we mean the impromptu creation of a scene with lines and action extemporized as the scene progresses. Different directors for different groups allow varying degrees of preparation. TV's popular *Whose Line is it, Anyway?* demands on-the-spot performance of very experienced professionals. An elementary language arts teacher may spend a significant amount of time discussing plot and character elements with primary students before actual scenes are improvised. The improvisation may be performed before an understanding audience or before one director. It may be an end unto itself or the springboard of a finished product such as those of *The Second City's Story Theatre*.

How can I use improv?

For those new to improvisation, know that it can be used as an individual activity to fill time (sponges, in educational terms) or as an instructional method to teach students dramatic concepts or how to think creatively on their feet. As such, we feel that improv is not only fun but also invaluable! And our students think so, too.

We have found that keeping up a fast pace contributes to the effectiveness of the activity. Keith Johnstone always says, *"don't be prepared,"* and this is extremely important to emphasize, as beginning players tend to feel that more careful planning makes for better scenes. We always stress that improv is a process, not necessarily an end in itself. As such, **participating** is the key factor, not being clever. Also there is a fine line between judging an improv as a successful **performance** and critiquing the **process**. In general, when the group is new, it is very important to focus on the **process** rather than the **product**. Make certain that participants do not feel that they will be "graded" for anything other than doing their best. Improv must be both fun and non-threatening.

What is side coaching?

The side coaching section indicates how a leader might suggest improvements in the activity as it is going on. The action of the game does not stop or slow down for coaching, just as it would not slow down in a basketball game. Students soon get used to having — and acting on — that "little voice" in their ear as they perform.

Side coaching ideas are followed by exclamation marks in this book, but may be spoken in any way the director thinks appropriate.

Side coaching concepts may be introduced before playing improv games, or the director may just start side coaching. If players stop to listen, the director says, "Just keep on; listen to me, but don't look." "I'm like your conscience; listen to me and try to do what I say." "Keep going."

What are the improv guidelines?

Regardless of the methods or goals of specific improvisations, there are a few guidelines that most improvisationists use.

Just Do It. Agree. Don't Block. Improvisation depends upon teamwork and playing off one another. Refusing to play or changing the ideas is called blocking and does not carry the improv forward. Accept the first idea offered.

Have Fun. Remember, improvs are a *fun* way to explore the abilities of one's self and fellow players, the group's dynamics, and of theatre. Follow the rules, follow the time limits, and share with your partners. Relax and have a good time. Improvs are not judged — participation is.

Keep it Appropriate. Improv depends on everyone — participants and audience alike — having a good time without worrying about being offended or hurt.

Therefore, there should be no profanity, obscenity, inappropriate references, hurtful statements, or cruelty. Everyone participating should feel comfortable.

Did you make up all the games and lists?

Many of the games are Justine's original ideas. Others have come to us from sources long forgotten — the "Improv Grapevine," if you will. Others are classics we learned in college with no origin given. The lists came entirely from our own imaginations, the creativity of our students, and many hours with a dictionary. We usually start an improv session with a player-generated list on the chalkboard.

Our own personal children, Nick Zanjani and Chris Kelley, spared us (or themselves) the embarrassment of sounding too old with their own contributions.

We encourage you to add to the lists from your own creativity and that of your players.

Talking the Theatre Talk

Theatre terms to know
(Including terms specific to this book)

Blocking (improv): Refusing to play, changing the ideas offered, or any action in an improv that does not carry the improv forward.

Blocking (play production): The management of physical action in the playing space. What part of the stage is used and why, the use of props and furniture, and the ways players move in the playing space are all part of blocking.

B-M-E: The basic plot elements of beginning-middle-end are abbreviated to B-M-E. (See below.)

Conventions: The practices that make improvisations and theatrical productions successful for both actors and audience. Speaking loudly enough to be heard by fellow players and audience, facing the audience most of the time, and giving and taking focus are all conventions.

Climax: The moment of greatest dramatic intensity; the turning point in the action.

Crisis: A moment of high dramatic intensity; a turning point in the action, usually followed by a decrease in suspense. (The final crisis is the *climax*.)

Denouement (day-noo-mah): The unraveling of the plot, following the climax, in which the players show how and why everything turned out as it did. A denouement is unnecessary for many short improvs.

Director: Group leaders, teachers, or play directors. Players may also serve as directors for games.

Ensemble: A group constituting an organic whole or working together for a single effect.

Endowment: A player is "given" an attribute by others and has to discover and/or adapt to it.

Exposition: The background information that reveals "how it all began;" namely, what happened prior to the time covered in the improv, what the characters are like, and what situation has arisen that will lead to a problem that must be solved.

Focus: The person or thing that receives the attention of both the players and the audience. Focus shifts throughout an improv.

Inciting incident (or episode): The incident that changes the story forever. The point at which there is no turning back in the story; things will never be the same.

Players: The participants in the improvs. Players may be actors or members of a recreational group.

Playing space: The area in which you perform, be it a stage, raised platform, or part of the room.

Plot: The series of events or episodes that make up the action of the improv. (Includes exposition, inciting incident, rising action, climax, and denouement [optional].)

Rising action: The series of events, preceding the climax, which intensify the conflict and, thereby, create a feeling of suspense about the outcome.

Setting: The background time, place, weather, and circumstances in which the events in an improv take place.

Plot: a beginning, a middle, and an ending

Whether it is Shakespeare, *Saturday Night Live*, or your own improv, plot is important.

The beginning contains the *exposition* which establishes *who*, *where*, *when*, and *while*. Most improvisation requires that the information be delivered quickly and concisely. For improvs that start immediately, the first player must give as much information to fellow players as possible. The beginning ends with the *inciting incident* or introduction of the problem.

The middle contains the *rising action*, which is the action which leads up to a *crisis*. Longer improvs may have several crises, each followed by a reduction in dramatic intensity, or *falling action*, which then leads into another increase in intensity and crisis.

The ending contains the final crisis — the moment of greatest dramatic intensity — which is called the *climax*. Improvs often end immediately after the climax. They may, however, offer the resolution and tying up of loose ends afforded with a *denouement*.

Groups: What, How, and When

Group composition

How does one arrive at the subgroups for games? Changing subgroup composition allows players to work with people they might not work with otherwise, but how do we get groups that are comfortable and work well together to change? Here are a few of our tricks.

Choose your own group: This technique is great with new players. It adds a level of comfort to the often uncomfortable or threatening idea of improvisation.

Work with a group that has one person you haven't worked with before: While allowing players to work with some people who are familiar, it allows them to expand their working relationships to include others in the large group.

Number off: Simple, but it works. Decide on the size of the subgroups you need. Divide the total number of players by the number of players in a subgroup. Have players number off into the number of subgroups you need. Then all ones work together, all twos work together, etc. If there are remainders, have them work with a group of their choosing or your assignment.

Assign groups: Why not? Especially after the large group has worked for a while and you are familiar with the individual members' styles. This technique can lead to magic.

Group size

Most of the games in this book are written to accommodate a large group of twenty-four to forty players. More than that, and playing time with smaller subgroups becomes unwieldy; fewer than that, and there often aren't enough to divide into larger subgroups. Subgroups (noted as "players" on the game pages) are as few as one and as many as six. *These numbers are just suggestions*; individual directors may choose to use smaller or larger subgroups to accommodate their own large group and players' skills.

Performance order

"May we go first? Let us be first, oh, please!" We have discovered that deciding on performance order before the first improv leaves little room for anguish later. Eager volunteers to improv in front of the large group are music to any director's ears, but sorting through the volunteers can be as difficult as assigning reluctant players. Here are some tricks to try.

Volunteering: "Who wants to go first?" The first hand that pops up goes. "Next?" The next hand, and so forth. (Don't forget to write them down!)

Assigning: Alphabetically by last — or first —name of a group's representative. The first group to go was the last group in the previous improv.

Random: "Choose a number between one and twenty-five." Draw from facedown, numbered index cards. Draw numbered ping-pong balls from a paper bag.

Combination of techniques.

Sample Games, Lists and More Lists

Ready-to-print lists

In the accompanying CD-ROM, you will find each list in two ready-to-print versions. The first version is for the Avery 5160 label. The other is twelve to a page, with cutting guides so they are ready to copy and cut apart.

Sample games

At least one sample game is given for each list. Don't let it stop you from using the list for your own games.

Lists next to games

Each list is printed on the page directly following the game (or games) the list goes with. Some games are easiest to play with a closely spaced list that only the director uses (*Tell Me About the Time You, Hitchhiker, The Wacky Family,* etc.) The lists printed in this book are ideal for this application. For lists for individuals or groups to draw, it's best to copy them onto cards or slips of paper, or you can use the ready-to-print lists on the accompanying CD-ROM.

Do *Your* Homework

Read and cull

While we have used many of these games with all age groups, some of the games are not suitable for everyone. Even with suitable games, some of the words on the lists may not be right for all players. *You know your players.* Please read the game through for suitability for your particular situation. Check over the lists, too, for any words or concepts that might offend or lead to your players being offensive. It's easier to remove words from a list than to do damage control.

FYI, in Appendix 3, will tell you at a glance how many players a game usually uses and whether the game requires equipment. *FYI* will also give information about preparation and playing times.

Guide to the Visual References in This Book

(Found in the game page information bar.)

Five Ws and an H

Journalism students are always told to remember the who, what, when, where, and how. We like to think that improv students need to learn to show the who, where, what, when, while, and how of a particular scene. Not all scenes are dependent on all of these attributes, but these may be used in many different ways. The top of the game page information bar indicates which W or H the game emphasizes. For reference, here are some hints on these essentials.

Who

Personal characteristics, emotions, occupations, attitudes, and physical attributes.

Where

Places where the scenes occur: rooms, enclosed spaces, vehicles, etc.

What

The plot as inspired by the beginning, middle, end, and conflicts. *What* can also be influenced by titles and plot ideas.

When

The time period in which the scene takes place.

While

What kind of weather might influence the scene? What is happening around the scene (revolution, power blackout, etc.)?

How

The style or genre in which the scene occurs.

Note: Some of the games don't have a W or H indicated in the margin. These are simply warm-up games for which there is no category.

Budgeting time for the games

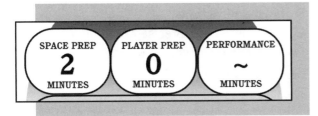

All of the times given are suggestions only. Improv leaders should tailor the time requirements of the exercises to fit their groups' needs.

Space prep

Some games require configuring the playing space. This may be as simple as arranging chairs in a circle for the group, or as complicated as creating a restaurant with three tables. The space prep box tells approximately how many minutes this activity will take.

Player prep

Some of the games require players to start immediately (noted with a zero), others allow players to prepare. *Note:* Preparation does not mean rehearsal —just deciding who should play which role, how the scene should end, etc. We have found that the less prep time, the more spontaneous and effective the idea generation and comfort level. However, directors may choose to allow for more time depending on the group's comfort level.

Performance time

Some games require a performance to be over within a certain amount of time, others are open-ended and allow the game to continue to its logical ending. Unless noted (such as in *Tell Me about the Time You*) timekeeping is casual and the games may end in *approximately* the time noted.

Use these for ...
the director's ulterior motives

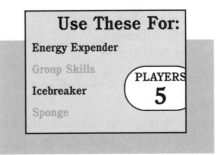

The "Use These For" list pinpoints how games can be used to achieve a director's goals for the exercise. The categories that apply to the game are in black.

Energy expenders

Just what the category says, energy expenders are active games that require running or other energetic movement. Often players perceive these as just plain fun; little do they know that they also are getting "dramatic benefits." Energy expenders are often *energy builders.* If they are played for a brief time when energy seems low, they can actually enhance the physical and mental energy of players.

Icebreakers

These games are particularly good for new groups or groups with new members.

Group skills

Each one of these games requires groups to work together well. Communication and give-and-take are essential for the games to work. Usually players intuitively know how to make these games work well. If necessary, the director will use side coaching or the critique and evaluation period to emphasize how the game could have been played better.

Sponge

Just as a sponge absorbs liquid — and can keep doing so, these games absorb indefinite amounts of time. Have a player who is late? Finish regular work early? Use a sponge. They can start and stop at will.

Players and equipment

Players

This number indicates the optimum number of players for the game. Games may be played with more or fewer players as the size of the full group, the experience of the players, and the needs of the game dictate.

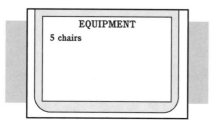

Equipment

In addition to a group/class list, the lists and the container with the copied and cut-apart lists, if applicable, accompanying the game that many directors find convenient, the equipment section notes other items that directors need to have on hand for the game to work at its best.

Teach and practice skills

Some of these games' teach and practice categories are exclusively for drama teachers, but many games speak to universal group attributes such as concentration, creativity, following directions, group dynamics, listening and silence, non-vocal communication, observation, and spontaneity. Use the accompanying charts to help select games to teach or practice specific skills. Skills that are taught and practiced in the game are in black.

> **Teach and Practice:**
> Blocking and Conventions
> Characterization
> Concentration
> Creativity
> Ensemble Acting
> Following Directions
> Group Dynamics
> Listening and Silence
> Memorization
> Non-vocal Communication
> Observation
> Physical Control
> Plot Structure
> Spontaneity

Blocking and conventions

Use of stage areas and the conventions of theatre (speaking loudly, facing the audience, etc.) are stressed in these games.

Characterization

Building believable characters is the key to these games.

Concentration

Paying close attention to the task at hand and to fellow players is required in these games.

Creativity

Thinking in unusual and even personally risky ways is encouraged in these games. The reward is acceptance and appreciation of each player's work.

Ensemble acting

The give-and-take and consideration for the individuals in the group, as well the group's effort, are important in these games.

Following directions

Close attention and precise execution of directions are what make these games work.

Group dynamics

These games have no stars. Players must work together to make everything come out right. Waiting one's turn is often very important.

Listening and silence

Attentive listening is important. Quietly waiting and appreciating the work of others is essential.

Memorization

These games hone memorization skills.

Non-vocal communication

Body language and gesture are often as important as what is said. These games encourage the use and observation of players' non-spoken work.

Observation

What players see, what they have seen, and how they use observation are the keys to success for these games.

Physical control

Precise movement and physical accuracy are important in making these games effective.

Plot structure

Beginnings, middles, and endings that work are what make these games successful. A complete story in the time given is the goal.

Spontaneity

Thinking and acting quickly is the goal of these games. From just fair to wonderful: it's the in-the-moment work that counts.

Dot com

Improv Encyclopedia
www.humanpingpongball.com

There are some great resources out there on the World Wide Web. If you see an icon such as this one, you may find more information at the Web site noted in the icon. We can't guarantee Web-site information, as many sites update regularly, and some even vanish. These worked at the time of publication. Check out humanpingpongball.com for 394 improv games.

About the Accompanying CD-ROM

Print and cut lists

The *Improv Ideas* CD-ROM contains the applicable lists in this book in a format that allows one to print the lists as needed and cut them into strips approximately a half sheet wide by an inch and a half tall. There are twelve items per page. Just use a paper cutter or scissors to cut along the dotted lines. On the CD, the file names of lists that may be printed onto strips are indicated with an "S" (for example: Accents-S).

Labels

The CD-ROM also contains suitable lists in a format that allows one to copy directly onto Avery 5160 labels (three wide by ten high per page). Labels may then be attached to 3 x 5 cards or used in the format of your choice. On the CD, the file names of lists that may be printed onto labels are indicated with an "L" (for example: Accents-L).

Unless otherwise indicated, the file names of the lists on the CD are the same as the names of the lists as they appear in this book.

What do I do with all those cards and slips?

You'll soon have an embarrassment of riches and a new problem. You'll either have to toss the cards and slips after you've used them once or find a way to store them. Justine, who likes to have lists on 3 x 5 cards, finds that 3 x 5 card boxes are perfect for storing and accessing cards. And, it seems that there are always some around. Teachers abandon them; they are stacked up at thrift shops and garage sales; and even stationary stores put them on sale. Not enough card boxes when and where you need them? How about resealable bags? They fit flat in desk or file drawers or even in hanging file folders. Mary Ann likes to photocopy her lists onto heavy colored paper and cut them into the smaller strips. She stashes her often-used lists in short juice cups on her desk for easy accessibility for sponges and special kid requests. Her less-used lists on that precious paper are stored in videocassette boxes bought at a discount warehouse store. They line up nicely on a bookshelf, look nice with labels on the spines, and strips can be doled out directly from the box. With the apparent demise of videotapes, however, she worries about her supply.

Laminate your cards and slips to increase their professional look and useful life.

Before printing PDFs onto Avery 5160 labels, you may have to adjust your print settings. On the print screen, (PC) be sure that "Page Scaling" is set to "None" and "Auto Rotate and Center" is not selected. This will ensure that your labels print properly.

Games and Lists

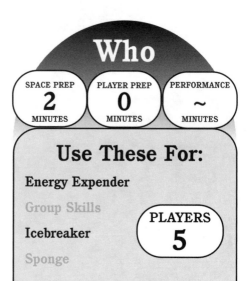

Who

SPACE PREP	PLAYER PREP	PERFORMANCE
2	**0**	**~**
MINUTES	MINUTES	MINUTES

Use These For:

Energy Expender

Group Skills

Icebreaker

Sponge

PLAYERS
5

Teach and Practice:

Blocking and Conventions

Characterization

Concentration

Creativity

Ensemble Acting

Following Directions

Group Dynamics

Listening and Silence

Memorization

Non-vocal Communication

Observation

Physical Control

Plot Structure

Spontaneity

EQUIPMENT
5 chairs.

Hitchhiker

Directions

- Divide into teams of five. Set up a "car" with two chairs in front and three in back.
- Decide if the game will be played using accents or attitudes.
- The first player serves as the driver and sits in the car. The rest of the players each think of, draw, or are assigned an accent or an attitude.
- One at a time the players enter the scene as hitchhikers. When they enter the car, each has a clear accent or attitude.
- As soon as each new hitchhiker enters the car, everyone in the car assumes the new player's accent or attitude.
- The exercise is over when all the hitchhikers have entered and changed the scene. The driver finds a motivation to end the scene.

Examples

Hitchhiker 1 is *tense*. Driver and Hitchhiker 1 fret about the trip. Hitchhiker 2 is *melancholy*; Driver, Hitchhiker 1, and Hitchhiker 2 display low spirits and a hopeless attitude toward the trip. Hitchhiker 3 is *terrified*. Driver, Hitchhikers 1, 2, and 3 all find terrifying aspects to the trip. Fear dominates until Hitchhiker 4 gets into the car. Hitchhiker 4 is the quintessential *laid-back* dude. Everyone chills for the rest of the mellow trip.

Side Coaching:

- Give and take focus!
- Don't all speak at once!
- Don't worry about your old character; it's different now!

Evaluation/Critique

- Did the actors all assume the new entrant's accent or attitude?
- Did they give and take focus?
- Was the ending motivated?

Challenges and Refinements

- After all have entered the car and assumed the fourth hitchhiker's attitude/accent, the driver finds a motivation to leave.
- The first hitchhiker takes the driver's place; the second hitchhiker takes the first hitchhiker's place, etc.
- The game continues as before with a new hitchhiker.
- Mix accents and attitudes.

Accents and Attitudes

Accents

African-American
Australian
Boston
British
Chicago
Chinese
Cockney
Ebonics
French
gangsta
gangster
German
Indian
Irish
Italian
Jamaican
Japanese
Jewish
Mid-Atlantic
Minnesota
New England
New York
Russian
Scandinavian
Scottish
Southern
Spanish
surfer dude
Texan
valley girl

Attitudes

aggravated	dull	jittery	shy
aggressive	easygoing	jolly	skeptical
agitated	ecstatic	jovial	smug
alarmed	elated	jubilant	somber
angry	embarrassed	jumpy	sophisticated
anguished	energetic	kind	sprightly
anxious	enthusiastic	laconic	springy
apologetic	exasperated	laid back	stiff
arrogant	excited	lazy	suave
athletic	exhilarated	lonely	submissive
authoritative	exuberant	loose	sunny
awed	fatigued	loving	supportive
bewildered	fearful	manic	surprising
bold	fidgety	meek	suspicious
bouncy	finicky	melancholy	tender
breezy	firm	mischievous	tense
buoyant	flexible	moody	tentative
burdened	flippant	mortified	terrified
casual	flirtatious	negative	threatening
cautious	formal	nervous	timid
chaotic	formidable	nurturing	tired
cheerful	frantic	obnoxious	troubled
cocky	frightened	open	unafraid
compassionate	grandiose	outspoken	unassuming
concerned	grieved	overwhelming	uncertain
condescending	grumpy	paranoid	unconstrained
confident	guilty	passive	uneasy
confused	halfhearted	perky	unrealistic
cool	halting	perplexed	unrestrained
correcting	happy	pitiful	unsure
creepy	hateful	poised	uptight
cynical	haughty	pompous	vacillating
dazed	heartbroken	ponderous	vague
debonair	hopeful	positive	vengeful
dejected	hopeless	purposeful	vigorous
delighted	horrified	quick	vulnerable
depressed	hostile	raving	wary
despondent	humiliated	regal	whiny
determined	hyper	relaxed	wired
disgruntled	hysterical	reliable	withdrawn
dismayed	incompetent	reserved	witty
dismissive	inconsistent	restrained	
disoriented	informal	reticent	
distracted	insecure	rigid	
distraught	intense	rude	
distressed	intimidated	sad	
ditzy	irrational	seductive	
dragging	jaunty	serene	
dreary	jealous	serious	

Who

SPACE PREP	PLAYER PREP	PERFORMANCE
0	**3**	**3**
MINUTES	MINUTES	MINUTES

Use These For:

Energy Expender

Group Skills

Icebreaker

Sponge

PLAYERS
5

Teach and Practice:

Blocking and Conventions

Characterization

Concentration

Creativity

Ensemble Acting

Following Directions

Group Dynamics

Listening and Silence

Memorization

Non-vocal Communication

Observation

Physical Control

Plot Structure

Spontaneity

EQUIPMENT
None.

The Wacky Family

Directions

- Divide into teams of five.
- Give the team a scene title with a blank for an emotional adjective. (For example, if the scene is "blind date," the scene title will be "The _____ blind date.")
- The team draws an emotional adjective to fill in the blank. They have three minutes to plan (not rehearse) their scene.
- The team has up to three minutes to play a scene that uses their adjective to define the overall mood of the scene within the context of the title.
- Critique team one and repeat the process with the rest of the improv teams.

Examples

- The *Blunt* family.
- The *Effervescent* First Date.
- The *Paranoid* Wedding.

Side Coaching

- Establish your role in the scene!
- Play for emotion!
- Show how that emotion affects your character!
- Use the emotion to develop the plot!

Evaluation/Critique

- Did the actors each have a character?
- Did the emotion help determine the plot?
- Did the title fit the plot?

Challenges and Refinements

- The scene starts immediately.
- Not all the characters have to have the emotion, but the adjective must be the *main focus* of the scene in order to act out the title.

Scenes and Adjectives

Scenes for Adjectives
File name on CD: Scenes4Adj

alien abduction
army induction
awards ceremony
beauty contest
birthday party
blind date
breakup
cruise
dance lesson
dinner at a fancy restaurant
dress rehearsal
driving lesson
family
family reunion
family vacation
first date
first day of school
first day on the job
graduation
makeover
manicure
marriage proposal
operation
prom
SAT
shopping trip
talent show tryout
therapy session
trip to the dentist
trip to the zoo
visit to grandma in the home
visit to the doctor
wedding

Adjectives for Scenes
File name on CD: Adj4Scenes

accident-prone
angry
anxious
athletic
bewildered
bouncy
cautious
cheerful
compassionate
confused
conservative
cool
creepy
cynical
depressed
disoriented
distraught
dull
ecstatic
elated
elegant
embarrassed
enchanting
energetic
exasperated
exhausted
exhilarated
exuberant
fearful
finicky
frightened
grumpy
guilty
happy
hateful
haughty
heartbroken
horrified
humiliated
hyper
hysterical
incompetent

irrational
jealous
jittery
jolly
jovial
jumpy
laid-back
lonely
loving
melancholy
mischievous
moody
mortified
nervous
obnoxious
outspoken
paranoid
perky
pitiful
poised
quivering
regal
relaxed
sad
serene
sleepy
sloppy
somber
suave
surprising
suspicious
tense
terrified
timid
tired
twittering
uneasy
vengeful
whiny
wild
wily
witty

SPACE PREP
0
MINUTES

PLAYER PREP
3
MINUTES

PERFORMANCE
3
MINUTES

Use These For:

Energy Expender

Group Skills

Icebreaker

Sponge

PLAYERS
3-5

Teach and Practice:

Blocking and Conventions

Characterization

Concentration

Creativity

Ensemble Acting

Following Directions

Group Dynamics

Listening and Silence

Memorization

Non-vocal Communication

Observation

Physical Control

Plot Structure

Spontaneity

EQUIPMENT

Assorted tables, chairs, and props as available and needed.

If I Were a Skunk

Directions

- Divide into teams of three to five.
- Choose one of the games in this book (*Film Critics, Hitchhiker,* etc.) to play.
- Each player thinks of, draws, or is assigned the name of an animal.
- In addition to following the other game directions, each player must *be* the selected animal in human form. The players may reveal their animals to the others in the scene.
- The audience guesses the animals at the end of the game/scene.

Examples

Film Critics: The People Next Door

Four players are chosen to act this scene. They are an *alligator*, a *buffalo*, a *dolphin*, and a *cow*. The dolphin and cow are an established docile but wise married couple who are worried about the alligator and buffalo couple who moved next door and are extremely noisy.

Side Coaching

- Show! Don't tell!
- Make sure to involve the animals' physical attributes as well as their imagined personalities!

Evaluation/Critique

- Did the characters display animal characteristics while still remaining recognizably human?
- Were there unusual animal combinations?
- Why did the combinations work (or not work)?

Challenges and Refinements

- As an icebreaker, play *Party Mix* (page 58) or *Party Quirk Endowments* (page 128) as animals. The players may be endowed with characteristics and have to guess what they are.
- Use as a warm-up for movement. The entire group moves like different animals (as in *Walking* on page 164) and switches animals at the director's signal.

aardvark
Abominable Snowman
alligator
alpaca
ant
anteater
armadillo
badger
barracuda
bat
bear
Bigfoot
blue jay
buffalo
butterfly
camel
cat
centipede
cheetah
chicken
chimpanzee
chipmunk
clam
cow
coyote
crab
crocodile
deer
dinosaur
dog
dolphin
dragon
dragonfly
duck

eagle
eel
elephant
elephant seal
emu
ferret
fish
frog
gazelle
giraffe
goat
goldfish
goose
gopher
gorilla
hamster
hawk
hippopotamus
hog
horse
human
hummingbird
hyena
ibex
ibis
iguana
jellyfish
kangaroo
koala
lemming
lemur
leopard
lion
llama

lobster
Loch Ness Monster
lynx
manatee
manta ray
mink
monkey
moth
mouse
opossum
orangutan
ostrich
otter
owl
panda
parakeet
parrot
penguin
pig
porcupine
rabbit
raccoon
rat
rattlesnake
raven
rhinoceros
roadrunner
robin
rooster
saber-toothed tiger
scallop
scorpion
sea lion
seagull

seal
shark
sheep
skunk
snail
snake
spider
squirrel
stingray
swan
tiger
toad
tortoise
turkey
turtle
unicorn
weasel
whale
wolf
wolverine
woodpecker
woolly mammoth
yak
zebra

SPACE PREP
2
MINUTES

PLAYER PREP
0
MINUTES

PERFORMANCE
~
MINUTES

Use These For:

Energy Expender

Group Skills

Icebreaker

PLAYERS
4-5

Sponge

Teach and Practice:

Blocking and Conventions

Characterization

Concentration

Creativity

Ensemble Acting

Following Directions

Group Dynamics

Listening and Silence

Memorization

Non-vocal Communication

Observation

Physical Control

Plot Structure

Spontaneity

EQUIPMENT
Assorted tables, chairs, and props as available and needed.

The Next-Door Neighbors

Directions

- Divide into teams of four to five. Set up two simple houses on-stage.
- One player (the new neighbor) draws an annoying personal habit.
- The rest of the players create a scene that starts at their house (House 1) with the family discussing the new neighbor who has moved in next door (House 2).
- The new neighbor from House 2 visits the family in House 1.
- The family welcomes the new neighbor to their home. As the introductions continue, the new neighbor gradually exaggerates his/her annoying personal habit.

Examples

- The neighbor has an *embarrassing itch* that he first tries to hide, but it becomes worse.
- The neighbor *giggles* inappropriately at all comments.

Side Coaching

- Gradually exaggerate your habit!
- The habit should seem "normal" until it gets out of control!
- Family tries to ignore the habit until it gets too obvious!
- Use the habit as a motivation for the rest of the plot!

Evaluation/Critique

- How did the neighbors manage to ignore the habit?
- How did the habit further the plot?

Challenges and Refinements

- There is more than one new neighbor, and each has an annoying personal habit.

Annoying Personal Habits

(File name on CD: APH)

blinking excessively
blowing gum bubbles
bumping into people
burping
chewing with an open mouth
constant hair combing
constantly primping
cutting in line
dropping things
elbowing people
excessive throat clearing
expectorating
falling asleep during a lecture or concert
fiddling with PDAs
fidgeting
fingernail biting
finishing other people's sentences
foot shuffling
giggling
gum chewing
head scratching
humming
laughing at one's own jokes
laughing at the wrong time
lip licking
lisping
loud nose blowing
nose picking
playing cards at inappropriate times
playing Hacky Sack at inappropriate times
pulling at one's own clothing
pulling one's own earlobe
putting on makeup in public
putting others down
rumor spreading
saying "and"

saying "like"
saying "uh, uh, uh"
scratching
self-serving flattery
smiling all the time
sniffing
snorting
spitting when talking
standing too close
staring
talking during a lecture or concert
talking in a nasal voice
talking in a whispery voice
talking on cell phones
talking too loudly
talking too softly
talking with food in one's mouth
telling dirty jokes
telling old jokes
thumb sucking
tooth picking
tooth sucking
tugging own hair
using lotion in public
using too much slang
wearing headphones
whistling
wiggling
wiggling foot when sitting
wiping nose on sleeve

SPACE PREP	PLAYER PREP	PERFORMANCE
1	**0**	**~**
MINUTES	MINUTES	MINUTES

Pass the Object

Use These For:

Energy Expender

Group Skills

Icebreaker

Sponge

> **PLAYERS**
> **Full Group**

Teach and Practice:

Blocking and Conventions

Characterization

Concentration

Creativity

Ensemble Acting

Following Directions

Group Dynamics

Listening and Silence

Memorization

Non-vocal Communication

Observation

Physical Control

Plot Structure

Spontaneity

EQUIPMENT

Chairs for players.
A neutral object, such as
ruler, ball, toy.

Directions

- All players sit in a circle.
- The director chooses a neutral object such as a ruler, a volleyball, or a teddy bear to pass around the circle clockwise.
- As the object is passed and received, the director calls out an attribute to which the players passing and receiving must respond. These may be called every three or four passes to keep the passing going and to observe variety.
- Directors may wish to use a checklist to keep track of attributes used.

Examples

- It's hot!
- It's cold!
- It's heavy!
- It's illegal!
- It's ugly!
- It's fragile!

Side Coaching

- Just do it. Don't plan your responses!
- Use your whole body, not just your face!
- Use all five senses!

Evaluation/Critique

- How did different recipients interpret the same attribute in different ways?
- Which senses were used most often?

Attributes

It makes you happy.
It makes you itch.
It makes you nervous.
It makes you sad.
It makes you sick.
It needs repair.
It's a family heirloom.
It's a handmade gift.
It's a long-lost item.
It's awkward.
It's beautiful.
It's been outlawed.
It's brilliant.
It's broken into bits.
It's bulky.
It's bumpy.
It's burning.
It's clear.
It's cold.
It's contagious.
It's cool.
It's creamy.
It's cuddly.
It's cute.
It's dangerous.
It's dead.
It's delicate.
It's dull.
It's dusty.
It's dying.
It's elastic.
It's fancy.
It's fat.
It's filthy.
It's fluffy.
It's foul.
It's fragrant.
It's frosty.

It's gigantic.
It's glamorous.
It's gooey.
It's greasy.
It's grotesque.
It's heavy.
It's homely.
It's hot.
It's icy.
It's illegal.
It's immense.
It's in pain.
It's large.
It's light.
It's little.
It's lumpy.
It's medicinal.
It's minuscule.
It's moist.
It's muddy.
It's musty.
It's ordinary.
It's peppery.
It's plain.
It's poisonous.
It's precious.
It's prickly.
It's putrid.
It's rotten.
It's rough.
It's sharp.
It's short.
It's silky.
It's slimy.
It's slippery.
It's small.
It's smoky.
It's smooth.

It's soft.
It's springy.
It's stale.
It's sticky.
It's stolen.
It's sweaty.
It's sweet.
It's tall.
It's thin.
It's ugly.
It's unusual.
It's very fragile.
It's very valuable.
It's wet.
It's your favorite plaything.
You are afraid of it.
You are strangely attracted to it.
You hate it.
You love it.
You need it.
You stole it.
You want to keep it.
You've seen it before.

SPACE PREP	PLAYER PREP	PERFORMANCE
2	**0**	**~**
MINUTES	MINUTES	MINUTES

Use These For:

Energy Expender

Group Skills

Icebreaker

Sponge

PLAYERS
Full Group

Teach and Practice:

Blocking and Conventions

Characterization

Concentration

Creativity

Ensemble Acting

Following Directions

Group Dynamics

Listening and Silence

Memorization

Non-vocal Communication

Observation

Physical Control

Plot Structure

Spontaneity

EQUIPMENT
A chair for each person in the group minus one.

Fruit Basket Upset

Directions

• All players — except one who stands — sit on chairs in a circle.
• The person standing calls out a category. All players who feel they fit in the category (including the player who is standing) get up and switch seats. They may not sit on the chair on either side of where they were last seated.
• Once everyone has moved, one person will be without a seat. That person calls out the next category.
• The play continues.

Side Coaching

• Move quickly!
• Do not push, shove, or step on anyone!
• You may not share seats!
• Accept when you're out graciously!

Categories

(Everyone who...)

believes in ghosts
can juggle
chews gum
collects something
doesn't eat meat
doesn't like chocolate
drinks diet soda
has a best friend
has a cat
has a digital camera
has a dog
has a secret
has a secret hiding place
has a younger brother
has an older sibling
has an unusual pet
has been bitten by a dog
has been in a movie
has been in a play
has blonde hair
has blue as a favorite color
has blue eyes
has broken a limb
has colored his or her hair
has done something dangerous
has e-mail at home
has flown in a helicopter
has gone scuba diving
has lived in another country
has met a movie star
has narrowly escaped death
has parachuted
has seen a play
has seen an alien
has traveled outside the U.S.
has won a first place trophy
is afraid of the dark

is an only child
is brave
is close to a cousin
is not afraid of snakes or spiders
is the oldest sibling
is wearing denim
likes *Lord of the Rings*
likes *The Simpsons*
likes anime
likes candles
likes cartoons
likes chocolate
likes horror movies
likes Italian food
likes Macintosh computers
likes school
likes science fiction
likes snakes
likes to eat meat
likes to read
likes to tell jokes
likes to tell stories
likes to wish on white horses
plays soccer
rides horses
skateboards
speaks more than one language
thinks dogs are better than cats
thinks MTV is better than Disney
thinks PBS is better than FOX
thinks school will be good this year
wants to be rich
wants to be a doctor
wants to be a lawyer
wants to be president
was born outside the U.S.
wears perfume or after-shave
would like to live in Paris

SPACE PREP
2
MINUTES

PLAYER PREP
0
MINUTES

PERFORMANCE
~
MINUTES

Use These For:

Energy Expender

Group Skills

Icebreaker

Sponge

PLAYERS
Full Group

Teach and Practice:

Blocking and Conventions

Characterization

Concentration

Creativity

Ensemble Acting

Following Directions

Group Dynamics

Listening and Silence

Memorization

Non-vocal Communication

Observation

Physical Control

Plot Structure

Spontaneity

EQUIPMENT
Chairs for players.

Name Game

Directions

- Players sit in a circle. The director decides the size of the circle or how often the process restarts.
- The director encourages the players to think of a friendly but accurate adjective that describes them and starts with the same sound as their first names. (The director may use the *Character Traits* list [page 24] to help stumped players.)
- The director chooses a player to start. The first player says, "I'm (own name), and I'm (character trait)."
- The next player says, "I'm (own name), and I'm (character trait). S/he's (first player's name), and s/he's (first player's character trait)."
- This continues around the circle with the players saying their own names and appropriate character traits and reciting the names and character traits of all players who went before them.

Examples

- I'm Jill, and I'm *joyful*.
- I'm Daniel, and I'm *daring*. She's Jill, and she's *joyful*.
- I'm Eleanor, and I'm *elegant*. He's Daniel, and he's *daring*. She's Jill, and she's *joyful*.

Side Coaching

- Choose your own word!
- The sound of the beginning of a name is not always the same as the letter!
- Pay attention so you'll be ready when your turn comes!

Evaluation/Critique

- Director compliments players on their choice of adjectives.
- Ask what adjectives might be used for the more difficult ones next time.

Challenges and Refinement

- Players choose a friendly adjective to describe the player next to them. ("This is Mary, and she's marvelous.")
- Players choose an adjective to describe themselves on the outside for the first round and one to describe themselves on the inside for the next round.

The Job Interview

Who

SPACE PREP	PLAYER PREP	PERFORMANCE
2	**0**	**3**
MINUTES	MINUTES	MINUTES

Directions

- Divide into teams of two. One player in each team is A, and one is B.
- A and B think of, draw, or are assigned an occupation (see *Occupations* on page 105).
- Each player draws a character trait.
- A interviews B for the job as both players gradually expand on their primary trait.
- The scene lasts three minutes.

Examples

- *Accident-prone* A interviews *cheerful* B for a job at McDonalds.
- *Exasperated* A interviews *lonely* B for a job as a school custodian.
- *Finicky* A interviews *paranoid* B for a job as an algebra instructor.

Side Coaching

- Make your emotions subtle at first!
- Gradually exaggerate your emotion!
- Use your emotion to propel the plot!
- Use your emotion to determine the outcome of the scene!

Evaluation/Critique

- Were the character traits clear and distinct?
- Did the character traits seem true to the characters?
- When exaggerated, were the character traits realistic, humorous, or both?

Use These For:

Energy Expender

Group Skills

Icebreaker

Sponge

PLAYERS
2

Teach and Practice:

Blocking and Conventions

Characterization

Concentration

Creativity

Ensemble Acting

Following Directions

Group Dynamics

Listening and Silence

Memorization

Non-vocal Communication

Observation

Physical Control

Plot Structure

Spontaneity

EQUIPMENT
2 chairs.

Character Traits

File name on CD: CharTrait

A

abhorrent
abominable
absurd
academic
accident-prone
acquisitive
active
admired
adorable
adored
affected
affordable
aggravated
aggravating
aggressive
agitated
agog
agonized
alluring
aloof
amazed
ambitious
amiable
amusing
analytical
angry
anguished
annoyed
annoying
antagonistic
anxious
apologetic
appalling
appealing
appreciated
apprehensive
approving
arbitrary

argumentative
arrogant
assuming
astonished
astonishing
athletic
attracting
attractive
audacious
awed

B

backstabbing
baronial
bashful
beautiful
believing
belligerent
benevolent
benign
bewildered
biased
bitter
blissful
blunt
bold
bored
boring
bouncy
bountiful
brainy
brave
brazen
breezy
bright
bubbly
buoyant

C

calm
casual
cautious

cerebral
charismatic
charitable
charming
cheeky
cheerful
cheesy
cherished
chic
childish
childlike
chilling
chivalrous
chummy
civil
coaxing
compassionate
competent
conceited
concerned
confident
confused
considerate
controversial
cool
cooperative
coquettish
cordial
courageous
courteous
credulous
creepy
critical
cynical

D

daft
daring
debonair
deceptive
decisive
dejected

delicate
demure
dependable
depressed
desirable
desperate
determined
dignified
disciplined
disconcerting
discreet
disheveled
disoriented
distraught
distressed
dogmatic
dopey
dragging
droll

E

eavesdropping
eccentric
ecstatic
effervescent
elated
elegant
elevating
embarrassed
eminent
emotional
empathetic
enchanting
endearing
energetic
engaging
enjoyable
enraged
entertaining
enthusiastic
envious
evasive

Character Traits

exasperated
excellent
excited
exciting
exemplary
exhausted
exhilarated
exotic
expectant
expensive
expressive
exquisite
extraordinary
extravagant
extreme
extroverted
exuberant

F

fabulous
faint-hearted
fair
faithful
fashionable
fatigued
fearful
felicitous
ferocious
fidgety
finicky
flippant
flirtatious
focused
foggy
forgetful
forgiving
forlorn
formal
frantic
frivolous
frolicsome
frugal
frustrated

G

gallant
gaudy
genial
genteel
gentle
giddy
giggly
glamorous
glib
gloomy
glorious
glum
gluttonous
goofy
gorgeous
graceful
gracious
grand
grateful
green (inexperienced)
gregarious
grieving
gross
grubby
grumpy
guilty
gutless
gutsy

H

handsome
harmless
harsh
hateful
haughty
healthy
heartbroken
heavy-handed
helpful
heroic
hesitant

hilarious
honest
honorable
hopeful
hopeless
horrified
howling
humble
humiliated
humorous
hurt
hyper
hysterical

I

idealistic
idiotic
idolized
ignorant
imaginative
immobile
impressive
impromptu
incompetent
inconspicuous
incredible
incredulous
indelicate
indescribable
indifferent
indiscreet
indispensable
indisposed
indomitable
indulgent
infallible
influential
informal
ingenuous
innocent
inquisitive
insane

insecure
insignificant
insipid
inspired
intelligent
intense
interested
interesting
intolerable
intolerant
intrepid
intriguing
introverted
intuitive
inventive
irrational
irrelevant
irreverent

J

jaded
jammin'
jaunty
jealous
jesting
jiggly
jinxed
jittery
jocular
jocund
joking
jolly
jolting
jovial
joyful
joyous
jubilant
judgmental
judicial
judicious
jumpy

Character Traits

K

kidding
kind
kittenish
knavish
knowing

L

laid back
late
lazy
leaderless
leaning
leery
legendary
leisurely
lethargic
liberal
likable
literate
litigious
lively
lofty
lonely
longing
loopy
loose
loved
lovely
loving
lucky
ludicrous

M

maddening
magical
magisterial
magnetic
magnificent
majestic
malicious
marvelous

meditative
melancholy
menacing
menial
mercurial
methodical
militant
mischievous
miserable
mistaken
modest
moody
mortified
mournful
muscular
mysterious
mystical

N

nasty
natural
neat
nebulous
necessary
nefarious
negative
neighborly
nervous
nervy
nice
nimble
noble
no good
noisy
nonchalant
nonconformist
nonresistant
normal
nosy
notable
noteworthy
notorious

O

objective
obliging
obnoxious
observant
obsessive
obstinate
obstreperous
obtrusive
obvious
occult
odd
official
old
omnipresent
opinionated
optimistic
ordinary
organized
original
ornery
outgoing
outrageous
outspoken
overjoyed
overwhelming

P

paranoid
particular
patient
peaceful
pedantic
perky
personable
persuasive
phenomenal
photogenic
picturesque
pitiful
poised
positive

practical
precocious
preferred
pretentious
prodigious
proficient
profound
prompt
prudent
punctual
purposeful
puzzled

Q

quaint
queasy
questioning
quick
quiet
quivering
quixotic
quizzical

R

radiant
ravishing
reasonable
recalcitrant
regal
rejected
relaxed
relieved
reluctant
remarkable
reputable
reserved
resourceful
respectable
respectful
restrained
reticent
revered
right

rigid
riotous
romantic
ruthless

S

scheming
scholarly
sensitive
sentimental
serene
serious
servile
shaking
shaky
sharp
shattered
sheepish
shifty
shining
shivering
shocked
show-off
show stopper
showy
shy
sleepy
sloppy
snide
solicitous
solitary
sophisticated
special
spiritual
stiff
stubborn
stunning
suave
subservient
subtle
suspicious
sympathetic

T

talented
teasing
temperamental
tempestuous
tense
tentative
terrific
terrified
thoughtful
thrifty
tight
timid
tingling
tired
tolerant
traditional
treacherous
treasured
trembling
trepidacious
triumphant
troubled
troublesome
truthful
tuneful

U

ultimate
unafraid
unassuming
unbudging
unconquerable
uncoordinated
undecided
understanding
understated
uneasy
unique
unlucky
unobtrusive
unparalleled

unpleasant
unprincipled
untiring
upset
upsetting
upstart
uptight
urbane
useful
useless

V

vacuous
vain
valiant
valorous
valuable
venerable
vibrant
vicious
victorious
vigorous
vindictive
virtuoso
virtuous
visible
visionary
visual
vital
vivacious
vivid
vociferous
volatile
voluble
voracious
vulgar
vulnerable

W

wacky
wakeful
wanton

wary
wasteful
wavering
weird
well-read
whimsical
whiny
wholehearted
wiggly
wild
willful
wilted
winning
winsome
wired
wiry
wise
wistful
withdrawn
witless
witty
woeful
wonderful
worried
wretched
writhing

X, Y, Z

xenophobic
yellow
yes man
young
youthful
zany
zealous
zigzagging
zippy

Who

SPACE PREP	PLAYER PREP	PERFORMANCE
2	**0**	**2**
MINUTES	MINUTES	MINUTES

Use These For:

Energy Expender

Group Skills

Icebreaker

Sponge

PLAYERS 2

Teach and Practice:

Blocking and Conventions

Characterization

Concentration

Creativity

Ensemble Acting

Following Directions

Group Dynamics

Listening and Silence

Memorization

Non-vocal Communication

Observation

Physical Control

Plot Structure

Spontaneity

EQUIPMENT
None.

●com American Film Institute
www.afi.com

In a Manner of Speaking

Directions

- Divide into teams of two.
- Each player thinks of, draws, or is assigned at least five clichés.
- The audience suggests a who and where. (Example: Bettors at a racetrack.)
- The improv starts immediately. Players improvise a two-minute scene with a beginning, middle, and ending in which they incorporate the clichés into the dialogue.

Side Coaching

- Establish who, where, and what right away!
- Develop at least one conflict!
- Use your entire vocal range to add variety to the clichés!
- You may repeat clichés for emphasis!

Evaluation/Critique

- Were you able to understand the plot when only a limited number of words/expressions were used?
- Did vocal variety make a difference?

Challenges and Refinements

- Expand or limit the number of clichés.
- Players prepare a one-minute scene using no more than five clichés.
- Try using the American Film Institute's top 100 movie song titles instead of clichés.
- Use any interesting list of your own in the same way.

Need a scene title?
Try a cliché!

Clichés (and Tired Phrases)

(File name on CD: Cliches)

A bird in the hand is worth two in the bush.

A day's pay for a day's work.

A friend in need is a friend indeed.

A penny saved is a penny earned.

A spoonful of sugar helps the medicine go down.

A stitch in time saves nine.

A wolf in sheep's clothing.

Accidents will happen.

All roads lead to Rome.

All's fair in love and war.

All's well that ends well.

Always look on the bright side of life.

An apple a day keeps the doctor away.

Are we mice, or are we men?

Avoid it like the plague.

Beware the ides of March.

Bloom where you are planted.

Break a leg.

Carpe diem.

C'est la vie.

Children should be seen and not heard.

Cleanliness is next to godliness.

Company, like fish, smells in three days.

Curiosity killed the cat.

Dead men tell no tales.

Don't bet the farm.

Don't bite off more than you can chew.

Don't bite the hand that feeds you.

Don't burn your candle at both ends.

Don't cast your pearls before swine.

Don't change horses in the middle of the stream.

Don't count your chickens before they've hatched.

Don't cry over spilt milk.

Don't eat yellow snow.

Don't fence me in.

Don't judge a book by its cover.

Don't judge a man until you've walked a mile in his shoes.

Don't let the cat out of the bag.

Don't let the sun set on your anger.

Don't look a gift horse in the mouth.

Don't make a mountain out of a molehill.

Don't put all your eggs in one basket.

Don't put off until tomorrow what you can do today.

Don't put the cart before the horse.

Don't sweat the small stuff.

Don't throw in the towel.

Don't worry; be happy!

Dressed to the nines.

Drinks like a fish.

Every cloud has a silver lining.

Every dog has its day.

Faint heart never won fair lady.

First impressions are lasting impressions.

Fool me once, shame on you. Fool me twice, shame on me.

Fools rush in where angels fear to tread.

For want of a nail, a kingdom was lost.

Genius is 1% inspiration and 99% perspiration.

Gilding the lily.

Girls just want to have fun.

Give a man a fish and he eats for a day. Teach a man to fish and he eats for the rest of his life.

Go west, young man.

Clichés (and Tired Phrases)

God helps those who help themselves.

Good as gold.

Grin and bear it.

Have a nice day.

He who hesitates is lost.

Hold your horses.

I got up on the wrong side of the bed.

I never met a man I didn't like.

I never promised you a rose garden.

I wash my hands of the matter.

If it looks like a ____ and sounds like a ____, it is a ____.

If it sounds too good to be true — it is.

If life hands you lemons, make lemonade.

If wishes were horses, beggars would ride.

I'll make him an offer he can't refuse.

I'm in the depths of despair.

I'm on cloud nine.

Is the Pope Catholic?

It's all the same.

It's in the bag.

It's raining cats and dogs.

It's time to face the music.

Jealousy is a green-eyed monster.

Keep it simple.

Keep on truckin'.

Kill two birds with one stone.

Laughter is the best medicine.

Let's call it a day.

Let's get the show on the road.

Life is life.

Life is what happens while you're busy making other plans.

Life isn't fair.

Lightning never strikes the same place twice.

Like a fish out of water.

Live and learn.

Live and let live.

Look before you leap.

Love will find a way.

Mad dogs and Englishmen go out in the noonday sun.

Marry in haste; repent in leisure.

Mind over matter.

Mind your P's and Q's.

Much ado about nothing.

Music hath the power to soothe the savage beast/breast.

Neither a borrower nor a lender be.

Never burn your bridges.

Not enough sense to come in out of the rain.

Nothing is certain except death and taxes.

One day at a time.

One rotten apple spoils the barrel.

Out of sight, out of mind.

Poor as church mice.

Qué será, será.

Question authority.

Read my lips.

Render unto Caesar what is Caesar's…

Rome wasn't built in a day.

Say it with flowers.

She knows him like the back of her hand.

She's dressed to kill.

Shoot first and ask questions later.

Show me the color of your money.

Silence is golden.

Skinny as a rail.

Clichés (and Tired Phrases)

Smile though your heart is breaking.

Smile, and the world smiles with you.

Smile. It makes people wonder.

Spare the rod and spoil the child.

Sticks and stones may break my bones, but words will never hurt me.

Stop pulling my leg.

Stuff happens.

Take it easy.

Take time to smell the roses.

Tempus fugit.

That really hit the spot.

That's a horse of a different color.

That's easier said than done.

That's how the cookie crumbles.

The apple doesn't fall far from the tree.

The eyes are the window of the soul.

The meek shall inherit the earth.

The only good _____ is a dead _____.

The race is not to the swift.

The salt of the earth.

The sun will come up tomorrow.

The unexamined life is not worth living.

There is no such thing as a free lunch.

There is nothing new under the sun.

There's a sucker born every minute.

There's neither good nor bad.

This too shall pass.

This will put hair on your chest.

Time and tide wait for no man.

Time flies like an arrow.

Time flies when you are having fun.

To the victor go the spoils.

To thine own self be true.

Today is the first day of the rest of your life.

Try not to rub him the wrong way.

Two can live as cheaply as one.

Up the creek without a paddle.

Virtue is its own reward.

Wake up and smell the coffee.

Walk softly and carry a big stick.

Waste not, want not.

Water, water everywhere, and not a drop to drink.

What goes around comes around.

Whatever!

When hell freezes over.

When in Rome, do as the Romans do.

Where there's a will, there's a way.

Where there's smoke there's fire.

Why be normal?

Why buy the cow if you can get the milk for free?

Winner takes all.

Winning is not everything.

You and what army?

You can bank on it.

You can lead a horse to water, but you can't make it drink.

You can't make an omelet without breaking a few eggs.

You can't teach an old dog new tricks.

You only have one chance to make a good first impression.

Who

SPACE PREP	PLAYER PREP	PERFORMANCE
5	**1**	**1**
MINUTES	MINUTES	MINUTES

Use These For:

Energy Expender

Group Skills

Icebreaker

Sponge

**PLAYERS
5-7**

Teach and Practice:

Blocking and Conventions

Characterization

Concentration

Creativity

Ensemble Acting

Following Directions

Group Dynamics

Listening and Silence

Memorization

Non-vocal Communication

Observation

Physical Control

Plot Structure

Spontaneity

EQUIPMENT

Assorted chairs, benches, and platforms as needed.

Yearbook Game

Directions

- Divide into teams of five to seven.
- Players think of, draw, or are assigned the name of a real or fictitious school club and are asked to form a frozen picture (tableau) that expresses the characteristics of the club.
- They have one minute to prepare the picture.

Example

The members of the *Creative Clothing Club* would modify their own clothing to make it "creative." A backward shirt, unevenly rolled up pants exposing uneven sock heights, arms inside a t-shirt, or a jacket wadded up inside a shirt to create an unusual silhouette.

Side Coaching

- What look would your group go for?
- Trust your partners and concentrate on your own look!
- Don't forget to pose so each member of your group can be seen!

Evaluation/Critique

- Did the frozen picture express the personality of the club?
- Was each of the members in character and memorable?
- Was the picture interesting to view in terms of variety in levels, body position, spacing, facial expressions, and gesture?

Challenges and Refinements

- Getting ready for the photo. The actors create a scene of the club characters getting ready for their yearbook photo.
- The Reunion. The same actors show their club character for the reunion photo ten years later.

Clubs

Alien Abductees Club
Anger Management Association
Anti-Club Club
Antisocial Club
Art Club
ASPCA Club
Backpacking Club
Bad Hair Day Club
Ballroom Dance Club
Big Dog Club
Canadian Club
Car Club
Cat Club
Cat Haters Club
Checkers Club
Cheerleaders Club
Chess Club
Civil War Re-enactors Club
Clown Club
Community Service Club
Computer Club
Cooking Club
Creative Anachronism Club
Creative Clothing Club
Detention Club
Ditz Club
Dog Lovers United
Drama Club
Dysfunctional Club
Ecology Club

Fantasy Lovers
Film Critics Club
Future Teachers of America
Geo Safari Club
Golf Club
Goths Anonymous
Gourmets of America
Greek Mythology Club
Green Party Club
Grunge Is Good
Hats, Glorious Hats
Hip Hop Club
Jocks Rule Club
Jocks, Not!
Jugglers Anonymous
Junior Achievement
Knitting Club
Magic Card Club
MATHCOUNTS
Mimes on Campus
Model Airplane Club
Model Rocket Club
Modeling Club
Nerd — And Proud of It Club
Outsiders Club
Paintball Club
Photography Club
Poets Club
Preppie Club
Puppetry Club

Rap It Up
Rebels Anonymous
Recyclers Club
Shoe Lovers Club
Short Pants at School
Sink or Swim
Ski Club
Slackers of America Club
Stand-Up Comic Club
The Arachnaphobes
The Music Lovers
The Spelling Bees
Thespians
Valley Girls Club
Video Gamers Club
We Love Our Planet Club
Weird Hair Club
Whistler Club
Who Cares? Club
Yearbook
Young Democrats
Young Republicans

33

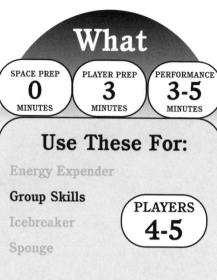

What

SPACE PREP
0
MINUTES

PLAYER PREP
3
MINUTES

PERFORMANCE
3-5
MINUTES

Use These For:

Energy Expender

Group Skills

Icebreaker

Sponge

PLAYERS
4-5

Teach and Practice:

Blocking and Conventions

Characterization

Concentration

Creativity

Ensemble Acting

Following Directions

Group Dynamics

Listening and Silence

Memorization

Non-vocal Communication

Observation

Physical Control

Plot Structure

Spontaneity

EQUIPMENT

2 chairs.

The Invention Of

Directions

- Divide into teams of four to five.
- Audience members call out the name of an unusual product, real or imaginary. (Use the *Cool and Unusual Products* list on page 35 for prompts if necessary.)
- The players take three minutes to plan a three- to five-minute documentary scene showing how this product came to be invented.

Examples

- The product may come from a well-known historical event (the egg beater in the Chinese earthquake).
- The product may be a fantasy event (dragons inventing fireballs).
- The product may be an offshoot of an existing product (how mixing bowls became helmets for soldiers in WWII).
- The product itself may be something unheard of, and the scene can show not only its invention, but its use.

Side Coaching

- Use your imaginations!
- Make imaginary connections!
- Use the shape (or imaginary shape) of the object to determine its use!
- Make this product extremely important to the world!

Evaluation/Critique

- Did the actors plan the steps in the product development?
- Was there a "eureka" moment when the product was finally discovered?

Challenges and Refinements

- The players immediately improvise the documentary scene.

Cool and Unusual Products

(File name on CD: Products)

3-D home movie cameras

anti-aging cream

anti-aging pill

antigravity shoes

anti-sweat soap

automatic climate control

automatic litter box cleaners

autopilots for cars

car that won't allow accidents

cloning machine

computers you can talk to

electric broom

elixir of youth

flashlight that needs no batteries

gourmet food machine

holo-deck

homework machine

in-ear language translator

instant diet pill

instant energy doser

instant face-lifter

instant freezer

instant heating oven

instant liposuction

instant muscle-building pills

instant umbrella

instant weight-gain pills

invisibility cloaks

love potion

massage chair

meal in a pill

micro-cooler

motorized skateboards

night vision glasses

non-caloric ice cream

non-wetable clothing

pen that switches colors of ink automatically

perfume dispenser that changes scents

permanent hair dye

permanent perfume

permanent pet sitters

personal air conditioning

personalized mind-reading key that opens
     everything you own

phone implant

phone ring (jewelry)

pocket computer

portable chef

portable mini water cooler

portable shower

replaceable organs

self-watering plants

smell-o-rama

sting repellent

television in mirror corner

television on fridge door

time machine

translators for animal languages

transporters

truly universal remote control

universal game board and pieces

universal money

universal electrical plug

x-ray glasses

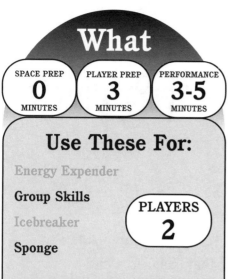

What

SPACE PREP	PLAYER PREP	PERFORMANCE
0	**3**	**3-5**
MINUTES	MINUTES	MINUTES

Use These For:

Energy Expender

Group Skills

Icebreaker

PLAYERS 2

Sponge

Teach and Practice:

Blocking and Conventions

Characterization

Concentration

Creativity

Ensemble Acting

Following Directions

Group Dynamics

Listening and Silence

Memorization

Non-vocal Communication

Observation

Physical Control

Plot Structure

Spontaneity

EQUIPMENT
None.

Conflict Game

Directions

- Divide into teams of two. Players designate themselves A or B.
- Players draw or are assigned a dilemma.
- Players get three minutes to plan a three- to five-minute scene with a beginning (introducing characters and the beginning of conflict), middle (acting out the conflict and adding small mini-conflicts or crises and/or a climax), and ending (resolution of conflict and scene).

Side Coaching

- Don't let the scene devolve into "he said/she said" or an irresolvable argument!
- Be creative with your solutions!
- Avoid boring compromises!
- Put action into your conflict!
- Really want your want!

Evaluation/Critique

- Was the crisis clear?
- Did the players come up with a creative solution?
- Was the solution dramatically interesting?
- How did the players incorporate action into their scene?

Bonus

- Players learn:
  - ✏ how conflict carries plot.
  - ✏ how conflict creates dramatic tension.
  - ✏ how to resolve a dramatic conflict.

For conflicts stemming from motivations, see *We Don't See Eye-to-Eye* on page 130.

Dilemmas

A wants ...	B wants ...
a cat	a dog
blonde hair	for A to keep the same hair color
dessert	to stick to her diet
to adopt a found puppy	to take the puppy to the pound
to answer the phone	to let the phone ring
to ask for directions	to figure it out
to be noticed	to disappear
to buy something	to save money
to confront a teacher	to let the problem go
to cover up evidence	to come clean of a mistake
to dine out	to go to a movie
to drive	to drive
to escape	to keep A prisoner
to go out	to stay home
to have a baby	to remain child-free
to leave the party	to stay at the party
to listen to country music	to listen to rap music
to make a prank call	to not make a prank call
to paint the wall white	to paint the wall bright blue
to pet the big dog	to be cautious
to pick up the snake	to run from the snake
to report a crime	to remain uninvolved
to see a funny movie	to see a scary movie
to see a romantic comedy	to see an action movie
to shoplift something	to pay for the item
to sing	to enjoy the silence
to stay up late	to go to bed
to stop at an accident	to go on
to take the subway	to take a taxi
to try drugs	to remain drug-free
to vote for the liberal candidate	to vote for the conservative candidate
to walk to the store	to drive to the store
to watch TV	to go to sleep
to wear a short skirt	to be conservative
to wear makeup	to be natural

SPACE PREP	PLAYER PREP	PERFORMANCE
0	**5**	**1**
MINUTES	MINUTES	MINUTES

Use These For:

Energy Expender

Group Skills

Icebreaker

Sponge

**PLAYERS
3-5**

Teach and Practice:

Blocking and Conventions

Characterization

Concentration

Creativity

Ensemble Acting

Following Directions

Group Dynamics

Listening and Silence

Memorization

Non-vocal Communication

Observation

Physical Control

Plot Structure

Spontaneity

EQUIPMENT
None.

Trapped

Directions

- Divide into teams of three to five.
- Players think of, draw, or are assigned an enclosed space.
- Players have five minutes to develop a one-minute scene in which one (or more) of the characters is trapped in the enclosed space. The scene must have a beginning, a middle, and an end.
- At the end, the situation of being trapped must be resolved in some way (rescue, escape, death, etc.).

Examples:

Ferris wheel: Three players: A, B, C. All players ride the Ferris wheel. When it is time to get off, A an B get off quickly; the restraining bar snaps back down, and C can't get out. C panics as he is hoisted into the air. It is no longer a fun ride. A and B watch — shouting advice and encouragement — as the car makes its circles. When the car comes to earth, A and B try to dislodge C. Finally C finds a small knob that releases the bar and comes back to earth triumphantly. The reunion is warm.

Side Coaching (Specific to Ferris Wheel)

- Really see your friend!
- Are you panicked, or are you just pretending?
- How high is the Ferris wheel?

Evaluation/Critique

- Could the audience tell where the players were?
- Was there a reason for the entrapment?
- Were the characters relevant to the plot?
- Were the characters unique?
- Did the scene have a beginning, a middle, and an end?
- Did the conflict have a resolution?

Enclosed Spaces

File name on CD: EnclSpaces

abandoned refrigerator

air vent

alley

attic

bank vault

baseball dugout

basement

bathroom stall

bathtub

box

broom closet

cabin

car trunk

CAT scanner

catacomb

cave

chemistry lab

closet

clothes dryer

coffin

computer lab

confessional booth

costume storage area

crawl space

crypt

darkroom

doctor's examination room

doghouse

dressing room

duffle bag

dumbwaiter

dumpster

elevator

empty swimming pool

Ferris wheel

fruit cellar

fun house

garage

glass elevator

gondola

grandfather clock

greenhouse

hollow log

hotel room

ice cream truck

jail cell

laboratory

laundry chute

locker

luggage

mad scientist's lab

mausoleum

meat locker

moving van

Murphy bed

new construction site

office cubicle

packing trunk

phone booth

photo booth

portable toilet

projection booth

recording studio

revolving door

sculptor's studio

secret passageway

sewer

shower stall

sleeping bag

storage room

storage shed

storm cellar

subway car

suitcase

swimming pool filter room

tent

theatre box seat

theatre lighting booth

tool shed

trash can

trash compactor

tunnel

tunnel of love

walk-in freezer

well

zoo cage

Where

Use These For:

Energy Expender

Group Skills

PLAYERS
Full Group

Icebreaker

Sponge

Teach and Practice:

Blocking and Conventions

Characterization

Concentration

Creativity

Ensemble Acting

Following Directions

Group Dynamics

Listening and Silence

Memorization

Non-vocal Communication

Observation

Physical Control

Plot Structure

Spontaneity

EQUIPMENT
A chair or bench.
Maps of basic stage
directions.

Exit, Stage Right!

Directions

- Distribute stage area maps (see *Appendix 3, page 193*).
- One player at a time is chosen to enter the playing area and cross to center.
- The player is given an entrance *as if* and an area from which to enter.
- The player enters as directed.
- After the player has entered and crossed to the chair or bench, the director gives an exit *as if* and an area through which to exit.
- The player exits as directed.

Examples

- Enter from Down Right. Cross to Center as if you are about to hear bad news. Exit Up Right as if you have heard good news.
- Starting at Down Left, exit Up Left as if you are going to hide.

Side Coaching

- Be aware of how you would use your body if you were actually experiencing the motivation!
- Use the chair or bench!
- Use a variety of pace that you think is appropriate to the mood!

For Directors

- Players should always note where the audience is on their stage maps.
- Scenes don't have to go together, but it helps if the entrance and exit are logical, especially for beginners.
- Stress the importance of motivating the movement.

Stage Area Map

Up Right	Up Center	Up Left
Center Right	Center	Center Left
Down Right	Down Center	Down Left

Audience

File name on CD: Ent&Exit

(Enter/Exit as if ...)

someone you don't want to meet is approaching.

there is a fire.

there is an earthquake.

you are about to audition for a play.

you are about to be interviewed for your first job.

you are about to hear bad news.

you are about to walk down the aisle.

you are afraid of the dark.

you are ashamed of yourself.

you are being called home for dinner.

you are being chased by a murderer.

you are coming out of a dark place into bright sunlight.

you are defusing a bomb.

you are frightened.

you are getting out of a crashed car — injured.

you are going on a blind date.

you are going to get help.

you are going to have your photo taken.

you are going to hide.

you are going to meet a lover.

you are going to meet your long lost cousin.

you are going to see your newborn for the first time.

you are having a really bad hair day.

you are hopeful of hearing good news.

you are jaywalking across a busy street.

you are late for an appointment.

you are leaving the scene of a crime.

you are looking for your lost dog.

you are looking for your lost homework.

you are lost.

you are modeling on a runway.

you are receiving an award.

you are running for a plane.

you are running for the school board.

you are running from a vicious dog.

you are sick to your stomach.

you are sneaking out of your house at 1:00 am.

you are trying to catch the bus that just passed you by.

you are trying to escape.

you are vanishing into thin air.

you can't take it anymore.

you don't want to be seen.

you got a bad report card.

you got all As on your report card.

you have been stood up for a date.

you have been walking all day and you are tired.

you have finally found your way out of a maze.

you have just been released from jail.

you have just fallen off your bicycle.

you have just put on a disguise.

you have just reached the top of Mt. Everest.

you have to get a tooth pulled.

you have to go to a funeral.

you have to go to the bathroom — badly.

you have to leave a party early.

you have to meet a deadline.

you just broke up with your significant other.

you just got off a roller coaster.

you just met the love of your life.

you just remembered something really important.

you just sat in something awful.

you just saw a rampaging tiger.

you just saw your significant other with someone else.

you realize you are not fully dressed.

you realize your clothes are on inside out.

you stole something.

you were lost but have just figured out where you are.

you wish you weren't where you are.

you won the lottery.

your feet really hurt.

your pants are on fire.

your room is on fire.

your shoes have been tied together.

you've been seen shoplifting.

you've just broken free from handcuffs.

you've just seen a ghost.

you've run away from an accident.

SPACE PREP	PLAYER PREP	PERFORMANCE
2	**0**	**~**
MINUTES	MINUTES	MINUTES

Use These For:

Energy Expender

Group Skills

Icebreaker

Sponge

PLAYERS
Full Group

Teach and Practice:

Blocking and Conventions

Characterization

Concentration

Creativity

Ensemble Acting

Following Directions

Group Dynamics

Listening and Silence

Memorization

Non-vocal Communication

Observation

Physical Control

Plot Structure

Spontaneity

EQUIPMENT
Sound makers; a list of sound prompts for the director, or ask players for a list of places and their distinctive sounds; a tape recorder and tape.

This Sounds Like the Place

Directions

- Director distributes sound makers if they will be used. Players are encouraged to use their voices, hands, etc. to make appropriate sounds.
- Group sits in a circle with eyes closed.
- Director suggests a sound environment and taps random players on their heads to add sounds to the environment.

Examples

- *An emergency room in a large city hospital.* Sounds could include: drip of IV, beep of heart monitor, paging for a doctor, moans, complaints, and rustles.
- *A haunted house.* Sounds could include: an owl hooting, wind, rain, evil laughs, creeks, groans, and chains rattling.

Side Coaching

- Make sure your sounds don't drown out others!
- Remember that there are background and foreground noises!
- You may include single words or phrases such as "Doctor?" "Paging Dr. Smith." "Help me!" "Where are you?" to add to the ambience!

Evaluation/Critique

- Did the overall sounds create an environment?
- Was a mood created?
- Were there changes in the mood?
- Did all the sounds support the sound environment?

Challenges and Refinements

- After the players have added sounds that repeat frequently or intermittently, sound is recorded and replayed.
- Use these environments as background for group improvised radio drama.
- Find and collect noisemakers to add to sound collections (rain sticks, broken glass in socks, bells, whistles).

Environments in Sound

File name on CD: SoundEnviro

aboard a pirate ship
airplane crash
airport runway
airport terminal
amusement park line leading to roller coaster
awards ceremony
backstage at a beauty pageant
backstage at a final dress rehearsal
backstage at a TV game show
backstage at World Wrestling Entertainment
backstage on opening night
bank
bank after hours
barnyard
beginning of a parade route
boring class
busy city street at rush hour
car wash fundraiser
casino
chemistry lab
church bazaar
church before a funeral
church before the wedding starts
coffee shop
computer lab
construction site
crowded high school hallway between classes
crowded laundromat
crowded subway car
deep-sea fishing boat
dentist office
department store fitting room
dining area at fast-food restaurant
dining room at exclusive restaurant
Disneyland
dog show
duck races
earthquake
elementary school office
elementary school playground at recess
emergency room in a big city hospital
factory assembly line
first day of kindergarten
football game at halftime
football locker room at halftime
Fourth of July parade
graduation ceremony
graveside funeral

grocery store checkout line
haunted house
helipad on hospital roof
high school cafeteria
high school prom
hoedown
hot air balloon festival
hydroelectric plant
Italian restaurant
kitchen in a home before dinner
library
little kids' soccer game
mad scientist's laboratory
monster truck rally
movie theatre before a blockbuster film starts
neighborhood on a summer Saturday morning
New Year's Eve party before midnight
newborn nursery at hospital
night at the farm
noisy classroom
nursery school
outdoor rock concert
passenger compartment of an in-flight transatlantic jet
pet parade
pet shop
popular beach at spring break
racetrack
residential street on garbage day
rock concert
scene of an auto accident
shopping mall, day after Thanksgiving
ski slope
sophisticated cocktail party
state fair animal barns
state fair midway
stock car races
stormy night
telemarketing work area
three-ring circus
thunder and lightning storm
tornado
trick-or-treating
wall at midnight — a target of graffiti
wedding ceremony
wedding reception

Use These For:

Energy Expender

Group Skills

Icebreaker

Sponge

PLAYERS
Full Group

Teach and Practice:

Blocking and Conventions

Characterization

Concentration

Creativity

Ensemble Acting

Following Directions

Group Dynamics

Listening and Silence

Memorization

Non-vocal Communication

Observation

Physical Control

Plot Structure

Spontaneity

EQUIPMENT
None.

SPACE PREP **0** MINUTES PLAYER PREP **0** MINUTES PERFORMANCE **<15** MINUTES

It Wasn't My Fault

Directions

- Players line up in two lines on each side of the playing area, facing each other.
- One at a time a player from one side then the other side takes Center Stage and gives an excuse for being late to class or not having homework.
- When players give an excuse, they go to the end of their original line.
- The pace should be fast.

Side Coaching

- Keep up the pace!
- Don't worry if you repeat someone else's excuse!
- If you go blank say, "pass," and go to the back of the line!

Evaluation

- Keep up the game until it lags. Then switch excuses for being late to class to excuses for not doing homework or just being late.
- The *Excuses* list provides ideas, but don't give too many or the players won't have enough! They are just "jogs."

Challenges and Refinements

- Go beyond the middle school and excuses. Add new categories such as cute names for dogs.
- Titles for new horror movies.
- Titles for children's books.

For more categories, see *Word Tennis Topics* on page 173.

Excuses

Excuses for being late

I couldn't find my car.

I didn't know it was Daylight Saving Time.

I forgot to write it down.

I forgot when I was supposed to be here.

I forgot where I was supposed to be.

I got a really important phone call just as I was leaving.

I got lost.

I had to take my brother to work first.

I had to visit my grandmother in the hospital.

I had to wait for my clothes to get out of the dryer.

I lost my car keys.

I ran into an old friend I hadn't seen for ten years.

I slipped on the ice, and no one would help me up.

I was carjacked.

I'm late?

My baby sister hid my shoes.

My car wouldn't start.

My dog ate my car keys.

My watch stopped.

We ran out of toilet paper.

Excuses for being late to class

I didn't feel like getting up.

I forgot and went to my fifth period class.

I got called to the principal's office.

I had to go to the nurse.

I left my book in math class and had to go back for it.

I left my book in my locker.

I thought it was lunch.

My locker jammed.

My science teacher kept me after class.

There was a stray dog on campus,
   and I had to get it help.

There were too many people in the hall.

Excuses for not turning in your homework

Homework? What homework?

I didn't feel like it.

I didn't understand it.

I forgot the assignment.

I had eight hours of homework in my other classes,
   and I thought you'd forgive me.

I had to go to the nurse.

I had to wash my hair.

It was too boring.

My brother wrapped his gum in it.

My dog ate it.

My hamster peed on it.

My little brother tore it up.

My mother used it for kindling.

My sister drew on it.

Our car broke down, and I had to walk
   three miles home.

Our cleaning lady accidentally threw it away.

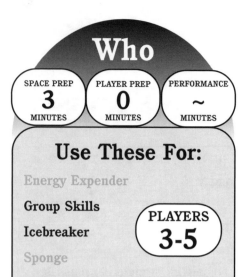

SPACE PREP	PLAYER PREP	PERFORMANCE
3	**0**	**~**
MINUTES	MINUTES	MINUTES

Use These For:

Energy Expender

Group Skills

Icebreaker

Sponge

PLAYERS
3-5

Teach and Practice:

Blocking and Conventions

Characterization

Concentration

Creativity

Ensemble Acting

Following Directions

Group Dynamics

Listening and Silence

Memorization

Non-vocal Communication

Observation

Physical Control

Plot Structure

Spontaneity

EQUIPMENT
Five chairs; optional desk.

Talk Show Game I

Directions

- Divide into teams of three to five. One player in each team is the talk show host. The other players are experts in certain subjects. (Use the *Experts* list on page 48.)
- One at a time, players join the host on his/her "show" and are interviewed about their areas of expertise.

Examples

- "Oprah" interviews experts on *carjacking, child psychology,* and *snake handling*.

Side Coaching

- Show how your character reflects your expertise!
- Interact with any conflicts in your areas of expertise (a policeman and a jewel thief)!

Evaluation/Critique

- How did the experts show their expertise? How well could they talk about it?
- How did the areas of expertise affect the players' characterizations?

Challenges and Refinements

- The experts interact with one another. For example, the psychologist convinces the carjacker to take up herpetology.

Talk Show Game II

Who

SPACE PREP	PLAYER PREP	PERFORMANCE
5	**0**	**~**
MINUTES	MINUTES	MINUTES

Directions

- Divide into teams of three to five. One player in each team is the host. The remaining players leave the room.
- Audience endows the four players as certain types of experts, but players are not informed.
- One at a time the players join the host and are interviewed. Since they do not know what they are experts in, the host must provide leading questions.
- Players try to guess what their areas of expertise really are.

Side Coaching

- Show, don't tell!
- (Host) Ask leading questions!
- (Guest) Don't keep trying to guess. Play along until you are fairly certain who you are!

Evaluation/Critique

- Which kinds of questions/comments helped the experts guess their areas of expertise?
- How did the players try to discover their expertise?

Use These For:

Energy Expender

Group Skills

Icebreaker

Sponge

PLAYERS 3-5

Teach and Practice:

Blocking and Conventions

Characterization

Concentration

Creativity

Ensemble Acting

Following Directions

Group Dynamics

Listening and Silence

Memorization

Non-vocal Communication

Observation

Physical Control

Plot Structure

Spontaneity

EQUIPMENT
Five chairs; optional desk.

Experts

auto body painter

baby-sitter

back flipper

backscratcher

bargain shopper

biblical scholar

blackjack dealer

bookbinder

bread kneader

butterfly collector

calligrapher

carjacker

cartoonist

charade player

checkers player

children's book illustrator

chocolate chip cookie maker

contortionist

cookbook writer

counterfeiter

creative excuse maker

diaper changer

dog breeder

dog walker

dogcatcher

dresser

exterminator

fast driver

file clerk

finger printer

fire-eater

flower arranger

folk singer

food taster

fortuneteller

funeral attendee

garage sale bargain-hunter

garbage collector

gossip

hair comber

hang glider pilot

horseshoer

hula dancer

impressionist

insomniac

juggler

jury member

knot tier

lie detecter

marathon dancer

marathon shopper

mask maker

mental math expert

mime

Monopoly player

MTV fan

mural painter

neat freak

paintballer

paleontologist

pancake maker

paperhanger

perfume tester

personal shopper

phone friend

phone solicitor

present wrapper

private back rubber

puppet maker

room decorator

Senior Olympian rollerblader

sewing machine repairman

Shakespearean quote quoter

shoe lacer

snake handler

street performer

sword swallower

tap dancer

tiger trainer

toenail painter

traffic weaver

translator

tree climber

trivia expert

tuna casserole maker

ukulele player

underwater basket weaver

unicorn wrangler

upholsterer

vacuum cleaner salesman

video game designer

video game player

Wal-Mart greeter

watermelon eater

What

SPACE PREP	PLAYER PREP	PERFORMANCE
3	**5**	**5**
MINUTES	MINUTES	MINUTES

Use These For:

Energy Expender

Group Skills

Icebreaker

Sponge

**PLAYERS
4-5**

Teach and Practice:

Blocking and Conventions

Characterization

Concentration

Creativity

Ensemble Acting

Following Directions

Group Dynamics

Listening and Silence

Memorization

Non-vocal Communication

Observation

Physical Control

Plot Structure

Spontaneity

EQUIPMENT

Assorted tables, chairs, and props as available and needed.

Fractured Fairy Tales

Directions

- Divide into teams of four to five.
- A member of each team thinks of, draws, or is assigned a title of a well-known fairy tale.
- Each team gets five to ten minutes to develop a slightly fractured version of the tale.
- The team performs the new version in approximately five minutes. Versions may be funny or serious.

Examples

- *The Little Match Girl* set in the bowery.
- *Aladdin* set in Iraq.
- *Hansel and Gretel* as runaways in modern day America.

Side Coaching

- Remember the elements of plot!
- Make sure you have a beginning, middle, and end!
- Choose at least one conflict to resolve!
- Decide how you are going to change the characters/plot!

Evaluation/Critique

- Was the plot coherent?
- Were the characters modified but recognizable?
- Was the original plot used to justify the new one?
- Did the new plot entertain?
- Was the plot amusing? Sad? Educational?
- Was the story worth fracturing?

Challenges and Refinements

- Combine two or more fairy tales.
- Place two or more tales in a modern or historical setting (see *Time Periods* on page 157).
- Choose characters from several fairy tales and put them in a contemporary situation.
- Choose characters from several tales and put them on a jury in a trial.

If a team is not familiar with the fairy tale they draw, they may draw another.

Fairy, Folk, and Children's Stories

File name on CD: FFC

Aladdin

Ali Baba and the Forty Thieves

Alice in Wonderland

Bartholomew and the Ooblick

Beauty and the Beast

Bluebeard

The Brave Little Tailor

The Bremen Town Musicians

Briar Rose

The Cat in the Hat

Cinderella

Clever Gretel

Dick Whittington and His Cat

The Elves and the Shoemaker

The Emperor's New Clothes

The Fisherman and His Wife

The Fox and the Geese

The Frog Prince

Genie in the Bottle

The Gingerbread Man

The Golden Conch

The Golden Goose

Goldilocks and the Three Bears

Goldnose

The Goose Girl

Hansel and Gretel

The Happy Prince

Harry Potter

Horton Hatches the Egg

Horton Hears a Who

How the Grinch Stole Christmas

Jack and the Beanstalk

Jack the Giant Killer

The Juniper Tree

The Little Engine That Could

The Little Girl that Trod on a Loaf

The Little Match Girl

The Little Mermaid

The Little Prince

Little Red Riding Hood

The Little Taylor

The Lorax

Many Moons

Mrs. Tiggywinkle

The Neverending Story

The Nightingale

One Eye, Two Eyes, Three Eyes

The Paper Bag Princess

Peter and the Wolf

Peter Pan

Peter Rabbit

The Pied Piper

Pinocchio

The Poor Man and the Rich Man

The Princess and the Pea

The Princess Bride

Puss in Boots

Rapunzel

The Reluctant Dragon

The Robber Bridegroom

Rumpelstiltskin

The Secret Life of Walter Mitty

The Selfish Giant

The Shoemaker and the Elves

Sinbad

The Six Swans

Sleeping Beauty

The Sneetches

The Snow Queen

Snow White and Rose Red

Snow White and the Seven Dwarfs

The Sorcerer's Apprentice

The Steadfast Tin Soldier

The Stinky Cheese Man

The Three Billy Goats Gruff

The Three Little Pigs

Thumbelina

The Tinderbox

Toad of Toad Hall

Tom Thumb

The Tortoise and the Hare

Twelve Dancing Princesses

Two Bad Mice

The Ugly Duckling

The Wind in the Willows

Winnie the Pooh

The Wizard of Oz

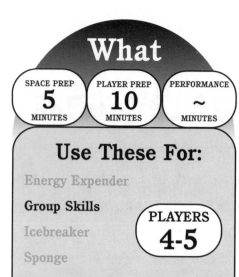

What

Use These For:

Energy Expender

Group Skills

Icebreaker

Sponge

PLAYERS 4-5

Teach and Practice:

Blocking and Conventions

Characterization

Concentration

Creativity

Ensemble Acting

Following Directions

Group Dynamics

Listening and Silence

Memorization

Non-vocal Communication

Observation

Physical Control

Plot Structure

Spontaneity

EQUIPMENT

Assorted tables, chairs, and props as available and needed.

What If

Directions

- Divide into teams of four to five.
- Decide on the approximate playing time of the scene before starting.
- Each team draws one *Fairy Tale Question*.
- Each team casts characters.
- The team takes about ten minutes to develop a plot that eventually answers the *Fairy Tale Question*.

Examples

- *What if Cinderella's father hadn't died?* Cinderella helps her father out of a potentially devastating marriage to a gold digger.
- *What if Aladdin hadn't found the magic lamp?* Aladdin is trapped underground until he finds an underground river, swims to freedom, and exacts his revenge on the wicked magician posing as his uncle.

Side Coaching

- Make sure you develop your plot!
- Make sure everyone has a character that furthers the plot!
- Answer the question!

Evaluation/Critique

- Is the original story obviously the basis for this diversion?
- Is the question answered?
- Is the new plot dramatically interesting?
- Does the plot have a beginning, a middle, and an end?
- Is the question resolved?

If a team is not familiar with the fairy tale they draw, they may draw another.

Fairy Tale Questions

File name on CD: FTQ

Aladdin and the Lamp: What if the lamp only produced a small elf?

Ali Baba and the Forty Thieves: What if Ali Baba's uncle had been generous and kind?

Alice in Wonderland: What if the Queen really beheaded Alice?

Beauty and the Beast: What if Beauty had rejected the Beast?

Beauty and the Beast: What if the Beast had eaten Beauty?

Bluebeard: What if none of Bluebeard's wives had been curious?

The Brave Little Tailor: What if the tailor had only killed *one* fly? Who would have thought him brave?

The Bremen Town Musicians: What if, in addition to the musicians, there really was a ghost?

The Cat in the Hat: What if the boy's parents came home, found the mess, and had him referred to a psychiatrist?

Chicken Little: What if the sky, in the form of an asteroid, really was falling on Chicken Little?

Cinderella: What if Cinderella's father hadn't died?

Cinderella: What if Cinderella's stepmother had been nice?

Cinderella: What if Cinderella's stepsisters really had been more beautiful than she?

The Fisherman and His Wife: What if the fisherman's wife really did get to be God?

The Frog Prince: What if the princess turned into a frog when she kissed the frog prince?

The Gingerbread Man: What if the gingerbread man was poisonous, and everybody knew it?

Goldilocks and the Three Bears: What if the bears thought Goldilocks was a beauty product salesperson?

Goldilocks and the Three Bears: What if the three bears had eaten Goldilocks?

Hansel and Gretel: What if the story were set in Japan? Would the house have been made of seaweed?

Hansel and Gretel: What if the witch was a vegetarian?

Horton Hatches the Egg: What if Horton organized everyone to take turns with the egg?

Horton Hears a Who: What if the Whos were larger and the earth smaller? What if the Whos heard Horton?

How the Grinch Stole Christmas: What if the Grinch was really misunderstood, and Max (the dog) used him as a front for evil deeds?

Fairy Tale Questions

Jack and the Beanstalk: What if the beanstalk grew along the ground instead of up?

Jack and the Beanstalk: What if the giant had eaten Jack?

King Midas: What if King Midas hadn't had the curse reversed?

The Little Engine that Could: What if the mountain was Mt. Everest?

The Little Match Girl: What if it were "The Little *Math* Girl"?

The Little Match Girl: What if the Little Match Girl used her last matches to help start a fire in a garbage can?

The Little Mermaid: What if the Little Mermaid and the prince had lived happily ever after?

The Little Mermaid: What if the prince was the one to fall in love with the mermaid and joined her underwater?

Little Red Riding Hood: What if Little Red Riding Hood had done what her mother told her?

Little Red Riding Hood: What if Little Red Riding Hood hadn't been rescued from the wolf?

Many Moons: What if the magicians actually found a way to give the princess the moon?

Peter and the Wolf: How would the plot be different if the music was rock or popular rather than the familiar classic?

Peter Rabbit: What if Farmer McGreggor caught rabbits for animal testing of makeup products?

The Pied Piper: What if children had refused to follow the Pied Piper?

Pinocchio: What if Pinocchio hadn't come alive, but Gepetto thought he had?

The Princess and the Pea: What if the queen had been nice to the princess?

The Princess and the Pea: What if the real princess hadn't felt the pea?

Puss in Boots: What if, after his first success, Puss hired himself out as a makeover consultant?

Rapunzel: What if Rapunzel's hair hadn't grown?

Rapunzel: What if the pregnant woman wanted carrots instead of rampion?

Rumpelstilskin: What if the maiden's mother had not tried to fool the prince?

Rumplestilskin: What if the princess hadn't guessed Rumpelstilskin's name?

The Secret Life of Walter Mitty: What if it were Mrs. Mitty who daydreamed, and Walter was an old stickler for reality?

The Shoemaker and the Elves: What if the elves were nudists and didn't want clothes?

Fairy Tale Questions

Sleeping Beauty: What if Sleeping Beauty hadn't pricked her finger on the spindle?

Sleeping Beauty: What if the bad fairy hadn't made it to Sleeping Beauty's christening?

The Sneetches: What if everyone was happy with what they were and didn't care about stars?

The Snow Queen: What if global warming was the queen's main concern?

Snow White: What if Snow White had rejected the prince?

Snow White: What if Snow White hadn't met the seven dwarfs?

The Sorcerer's Apprentice: What if the sorcerer didn't come back, and the water kept coming?

The Three Billy Goats Gruff: What if the troll hadn't eaten the first two billy goats?

The Three Billy Goats Gruff: What if the troll was a toll collector for the king?

The Three Little Pigs: What if the wolf had puffed *all* the pigs' houses down?

The Three Little Pigs: What if the wolf just wanted to visit the pigs?

Through the Looking Glass: What if the story was based on Monopoly instead of chess?

The Tinderbox: What if the soldier was served by very clever poodles when he lit the fires?

The Tortoise and the Hare: What if the hare was very concerned about getting corporate sponsorship for his running?

Twelve Dancing Princesses: What if one of the princesses didn't like the kind of dancing the others did and wouldn't go with them?

The Ugly Duckling: What if it weren't a swan's egg but a dragon's egg that was in the duck's nest?

Winnie the Pooh: What if Pooh hated honey?

Winnie the Pooh: What if Pooh was allergic to honey?

SPACE PREP
0
MINUTES

PLAYER PREP
0
MINUTES

PERFORMANCE
2
MINUTES

Buddies

Use These For:

Energy Expender

Group Skills

PLAYERS
2

Icebreaker

Sponge

Teach and Practice:

Blocking and Conventions

Characterization

Concentration

Creativity

Ensemble Acting

Following Directions

Group Dynamics

Listening and Silence

Memorization

Non-vocal Communication

Observation

Physical Control

Plot Structure

Spontaneity

EQUIPMENT
None.

Directions

- Divide into teams of two.
- Each improv pair draws a famous buddy pair and either a title (*Film Titles* on page 61), or a place (*Places* on page 119), or an improv that uses two characters (*The Job Interview*, page 23; *Conflict Game*, page 36; *Opening and Closing Scenes*, page 108).
- The play starts immediately as the pair uses the real or imagined personality characteristics of the famous buddies to create a two-minute scene in which these characters interact.

Examples

- Adam and Eve in a jungle.
- Abbot and Costello in *The People Next Door*.
- Scooby and Shaggy solve the crime of bullying on the playground.

Evaluation and Critique

- Did the players play the understood characteristics of their buddies?
- Did the buddies have a relationship?
- Did the personalities of the buddies further the plot?
- Did the personalities of the buddies add to the mood (Abbot/Costello are comic while Othello/Desdemona are tragic)?
- Were the plot elements clear?

Famous Pairs

Aladdin/Jasmine
Androcles/Lion
Andy/Barney
Anna/King of Siam
Anne Bancroft/Mel Brooks
Anthony/Cleopatra
Babar/Celeste
Barbie/Ken
Barnum/Bailey
Baskin/Robbins
Batman/Robin
Bell/Howell
Ben/Jerry
Benedick/Beatrice
Bill/Hillary
Bill/Ted
Bogart/Bacall
Boris/Natasha
Briggs/Stratton
Brooks/Dunn
Burns/Allen
Caesar/Calpurnia
Caesar/Cleopatra
Captain Hook/Smee
Clark Kent/Lois Lane
Dagwood/Blondie
David/Jezebel
David/Lisa
Donald/Daisy
Dorothy/Toto
Edmund Hilary/Tenzing Norgay
Flotsam/Jetsam
Fred/Barney
Frick/Frack
Garth/Wayne
George/Barbara

George/Martha
Gilligan/Skipper
Hades/Persephone
Hamlet/Ophelia
Han Solo/Leia
Hercules/Megara
Hi/Lois
Holmes/Watson
Homer/Marge
Jay/Silent Bob
Joanne Woodward/Paul Newman
Johnny Carson/Ed McMahon
Johnson/Johnson
Kaufman/Hart
King Arthur/Guinevere
King Arthur/Lancelot
Lady/Tramp
Lancelot/Guinevere
Lassie/Timmy
Laurel/Hardy
Laverne/Shirley
Lerner/Loewe
Little Orphan Annie/Daddy Warbucks
Lone Ranger/Tonto
Lucy/Desi
Lucy/Schroeder
Luke Skywalker/Han Solo
Lunt/Fontaine
Mary/Rhoda
Mickey/Minnie
Mickey/Walt
Morticia/Gomez
Mr. Ed/Wilbur
Napoleon/Josephine
Nicholas/Alexandra
Noah/Noah's wife

Orville/Wilbur
Oscar/Felix
Othello/Desdemona
Ozzie/Harriet
Peter Pan/Tinkerbell
Peter Pan/Wendy
Peter Parker/Mary Jane
Porky/Petunia Pig
Rocky/Bullwinkle
Rogers/Hammerstein
Romeo/Juliet
Rowan/Martin
Roy Rogers/Dale Evans
Samson/Delilah
Santa/Mrs. Claus
Scooby/Shaggy
Siegfried/Roy
Simon/Garfunkel
Simon/Schuster
Smith/Wesson
Sonny/Cher
Sponge Bob/Patrick
Thelma/Louise
Tom/Jerry
Tristan/Isolde
Troilus/Cressida
Turner/Hooch
Ulysses/Penelope
Victoria/Albert
Wallace/Gromit
Walter Matthau/Jack Lemmon
Ward/June
Your mother/Your father
Your principal/Your teacher
Zeus/Hera

SPACE PREP
~
MINUTES

PLAYER PREP
~
MINUTES

PERFORMANCE
~
MINUTES

Use These For:

Energy Expender

Group Skills

Icebreaker

Sponge

PLAYERS
Full Group

Teach and Practice:

Blocking and Conventions

Characterization

Concentration

Creativity

Ensemble Acting

Following Directions

Group Dynamics

Listening and Silence

Memorization

Non-vocal Communication

Observation

Physical Control

Plot Structure

Spontaneity

EQUIPMENT
Nametags pre-printed with the names of famous people.

Party Mix

Directions

- Attach a nametag with a famous person's name to the back of each player as they enter the room.
- Players read the other players' names and react and interact with them as if they were that person.
- Players interact with others, although they do not know who they are supposed to be, always gleaning hints of their endowed identity from the other players.
- When players guess who they are they then "become" that famous person.

Side Coaching

- Show, don't tell!
- Don't give away each other's identities!
- Do give players good, but not too obvious, clues as to their identities!
- Do assume your character's physical traits as soon as you find out who you are!

Evaluation/Critique

- Which types of questions and introductions helped you to guess your character?
- Were other players' physical portrayals of their characters believable?

Challenges and Refinements

- After most players have guessed and assumed their roles, put them in a talk show situation. (See *Talk Show Games I & II* on pages 46-47.)
- Stage a news report or an awards presentation at which some of these characters are present.
- Stage a trial in which one of the famous people has committed a crime and some of the others are witnesses.
- Use the *Famous Pairs* list on page 57 to create pairs of players. The nametags would have both names with the wearer's individual buddy name highlighted.

Famous People

Abraham

Aladdin

Alexander the Great

Muhammad Ali

Ali Baba

Jennifer Aniston

Yasser Arafat

Aristotle

Jane Austen

Bilbo Baggins

Alexander Graham Bell

Osama Bin Laden

Ann Boleyn

Napoleon Bonaparte

William H. Bonney, a.k.a.
    Billy the Kid

John Wilkes Booth

Lizzie Borden

Brad Pitt

Beau Brummel

Kobe Bryant

Mr. Burns

George Bush

George Carlin

Jackie Chan

Charles, Prince of Wales

Cher

Chewbacca

Bill Clinton

Columbo

Christopher Columbus

Tiny Tim Cratchett

Walter Cronkite

Tom Cruise

Jeffrey Dahmer

Darth Vader

Diana, Princess of Wales

Charles Dickens

Donald Duck

Alfred Donner

Arthur Conan Doyle

Dracula

Bob Dylan

Wyatt Earp

Albert Einstein

Elizabeth I,
    Queen of England

Elizabeth II,
    Queen of England

Elvis

Leif Ericsson

Farmer McGreggor

Dr. Frankenstein

Frankenstein's Monster

Benjamin Franklin

Sigmund Freud

Gandalf

Gandhi

Genghis Khan

Goliath

Goofy

Rudy Giuliani

Anne Hathaway

Henry VIII,
    King of England

Sherlock Holmes

Jack Be Nimble

Jack the Ripper

Michael Jackson

Jonah

Michael Jordan

Carl Jung

John F. Kennedy

Joseph Kennedy

Kenny

Martin Luther King, Jr.

Nathan Lane

Bruce Lee

Abraham Lincoln

Lucy Liu

Jennifer Lopez

George Lucas

Martin Luther

Madonna

Malcolm X

Mickey Mouse

Joe Montana

Moses

Bill Murray

Noah

Rosie O'Donnell

Shaquille O'Neal

Obi Wan Kenobi

Jacqueline Onassis

Rosa Parks

George Patton

Eva Perón

Peter Pan

Peter Rabbit

Plato

Hercule Poirot

Harry Potter

Prince

Princess Leia

Sir Walter Raleigh

Dan Rather

Julia Roberts

Robespierre

Chris Rock

Sampson

Scooby Doo

Dr. Seuss

Shaggy

William Shakespeare

Bart Simpson

Homer Simpson

Luke Skywalker

Anakin Skywalker

Socrates

Stephen Sondheim

Spartacus

Britney Spears

Spiderman

Stephen Spielberg

Quentin Tarantino

Tinkerbell

Tiny Tim (the singer)

Tutankhamen, a.k.a.
    King Tut

Typhoid Mary

Victoria,
    Queen of England

William Wallace, a.k.a.
    Braveheart

George Washington

Oprah Winfrey

The Wizard of Oz

Yoda

SPACE PREP	PLAYER PREP	PERFORMANCE
0	**0**	**<10**
MINUTES	MINUTES	MINUTES

Use These For:

Energy Expender

Group Skills

Icebreaker

Sponge

PLAYERS
5

Teach and Practice:

Blocking and Conventions

Characterization

Concentration

Creativity

Ensemble Acting

Following Directions

Group Dynamics

Listening and Silence

Memorization

Non-vocal Communication

Observation

Physical Control

Plot Structure

Spontaneity

EQUIPMENT
2 Chairs.

Film Critics

Directions

- Divide into teams of five. Two players on the team are film critics. Three players act out the various films that the critics review.
- The critics think of, draw, or are assigned film titles.
- The critics comment on the films one at a time. They may identify a broad category (chick flicks, horror movies, worst films of the year) or discuss which films they like or dislike (thumbs up or thumbs down).
- As they establish commentary on the film, they identify a scene of the film to be viewed ("Let's see the stunning climax," or "This is the moment when the lovers first meet.").
- The critics narrate the action as the three players act out the scene until the critics "stop" the film and either call for another scene from that film or go on to the next film.

Side Coaching

- Critics, give specific directions to the actors about their characters and part of the plot! ("In this frightening scene the little boy discovers the murderer hiding in the closet with the boy's sister.")

Evaluation/Critique

- Did the critics provide the specific information for the actors to use?
- Did the actors capture the mood?

Challenges and Refinements

- The group chooses a film they find particularly interesting and have the actors perform more of the scene.
- The film critics choose opening, closing, and climactic moments.

Film Titles

Alien Invasion
Alligators in the Sewer
All Alone
All Around Me
Alone At Last
Anything to Win
The Asylum
At the Mall
Attack of the Killer
  Spinach
The Audition
The Barbershop
Behind the Blue Door
Behind the Door
Beyond Escape
The Big Town
The Birthday Party
Blame Canada
Blueblood
Breakdown
The Bridge
Bright Lights
The Broken Arm
Busted!
The Call from the
  Downstairs Phone
Cat People
The Chair
Christmas at Ground
  Zero
The Closet
The Clown's Revenge
Cops
The Crocodile Hunter
The Crypt
The Day It Snowed
  Raisins
The Day the Sun Went
  Out
Desperate Hours
Diamonds are a Girl's
  Best Friend
Diamonds are Forever
Diva
The Door in the Wall
Down the Mine
Earthquake

Evil under the Sun
Eyewitness
Fabulous
Fever
The Fire
First Date
Follow Me
Footsteps
The Forgiven
The Ghost of Room 112
Girls Night Out
The Glass Eye
The Graveyard
The Great Waldo
Green Light
Ground Zero
The Hand of Death
The Haunted House
Have Mercy
Heartland
Home Alone
The Hook
I Can Fix That
If You Only Knew
In the Attic
In the Cage
In the Closet
In the Jungle
Into the Past
Into the Woods
It
It Came from _____
It Came from Science
  Class
It's Not Easy Being
  Green
The Journal of Michelle B.
Jungle Fever
Justice Lost
The King of Everything
The Last Detail
The Last Train
Legends
Light of Day
Listen Up
The Locked Door
Locked In

The Lone Wolf
Losers
Lost
The Lost Homework
Make My Day
The Man in the
  Dumpster
The Manhole
A Midnight Walk
The Mirror
The Missing Agenda
The Mission
The Modem
Neighbors
Never Again
Never Alone
Night of the Comets
Nine Days
No Exit
Noonday Sun
October 31
The Old House
One Cold Night
One Hot Day
One Smart Cookie
The Operation
Orphans
Outrage
Outrageous
The Owl
The People Next Door
The People on the Roof
The Phantom
The Pharmacy
The Phone Call
Pigs Can Fly
The Pimple
Poison Rain
The Prince
The Prison
Quiz Show
Rear Window
The Roll of the Dice
Rubbed Out
Rumors
Runaways
Scandal

School Days
School's Out
The Secret
The Shadow
Smarter Than You Think
Someone is Missing
The Spider
Starry, Starry Night
Stuck
Submerged
Summer Camp
Summer's Gone
Sunday in the Park
Surprise Party
Thief of Time
Three Days and Two
  Nights
Too Beautiful for You
Too Late
The Tower
Train to Nowhere
Trapped
The Trophy Wife
Tsunami
The Two-Way Mirror
Under Duress
Under the Volcano
A Very Bad Day
The Virus
The Visitor
The Voices Behind the
  Wall
Volcano
We Are Too Late
What I Really Did Last
  Summer
Widow's Weeds
World Without Man
World Without Men
The Writing on the
  Bathroom Stalls

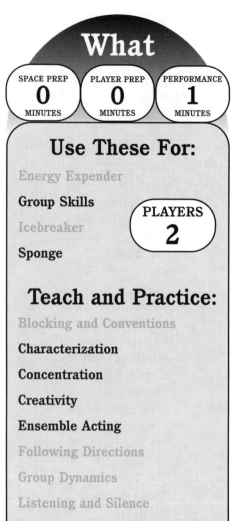

What

SPACE PREP	PLAYER PREP	PERFORMANCE
0	**0**	**1**
MINUTES	MINUTES	MINUTES

Use These For:

Energy Expender

Group Skills

Icebreaker

PLAYERS 2

Sponge

Teach and Practice:

Blocking and Conventions

Characterization

Concentration

Creativity

Ensemble Acting

Following Directions

Group Dynamics

Listening and Silence

Memorization

Non-vocal Communication

Observation

Physical Control

Plot Structure

Spontaneity

EQUIPMENT
None.

First Line, Last Line

Directions
- Divide into teams of two. Teams are divided into As and Bs.
- Player A is given a line to open with. Player B is given a line to close with.
- The audience supplies a location, title, or situation.
- Player A starts the scene with the opening line.
- The players develop the scene for about one minute.
- Player B ends the scene with the closing line.

Example
Player A draws "You won't believe what happened today." The scene develops into a litany of woes that develops into real-time problems (sink plugging up, slipping on a banana peel, being bit by a hamster, etc.) until Player B ends with his drawn last line, "Is it really over?"

Evaluation/Critique
- Did the players establish a coherent scene that incorporated both lines?
- Did the players establish clear characters?
- Did the players establish a clear sense of place?
- Was the plot coherent and consistent?
- Did the scene have a beginning, middle, and end?
- Was the closing line motivated?

Challenges and Refinements
- The American Film Institute has four hundred film quotes — many of which would make wonderful first or last lines. (Look them over first!)

First Line, Last Line

File name on CD: FirstLast

A penguin? Where?

A snake!

Anger will get you nowhere.

Are you all right?

Are you crazy?

Are you sure?

At last.

Bang, you're dead.

Behind you!

But it's so ugly.

Come in, come in.

Congratulations, you've just given birth to a ___.

Congratulations.

Did you hear that?

Do you believe in ghosts?

Do you hear what I hear?

Do you realize what you just did?

Do you see what I see?

Does that feel better?

Don't do that here.

Don't leave me here.

Don't let him see you.

Don't make me do it.

Don't talk to me like that.

Don't tell me that.

Don't throw that.

Don't touch me.

Don't touch that switch.

Don't touch the blue one!

Duck!

Fire!

Forget it.

Forgive me.

Freeze, right where you are!

Get your hands off me.

Give me that flashlight *now*!

Go away.

Guess what I saw on the way to work today.

He's in the next room.

Hide!

Hold it like this.

How can I ever repay you?

How many armed peasants did you say
     are out there?

How much?

I believe this is yours.

I can't get an outside line.

I can't go on.

I can't go through with this.

I can't see through this window.

I can't see.

I don't believe it.

I don't smell anything.

I don't want to go in there.

I feel dizzy.

I never saw anything like that before.

I never thought it could come to this.

I never want to see you again.

I never wanted to do it in the first place.

First Line, Last Line

I really appreciate this.

I spy with my little eye …

I think I'm going to throw up.

I told you not to do that.

I will never forgive you for this.

I will never speak to you again.

I wonder what would happen if I pushed this button.

If I told you once, I've told you a hundred times. No.

I'll never be able to repay you.

I'll never do that again.

I'll never forget what you've done for me.

I'll take door three.

I'm depressed.

I'm dying!

I'm hungry.

I'm leaving.

I'm not going to bail you out this time.

I'm so glad you came.

I'm sorry.

Is it really over?

Is that what I think it is?

Is this the end?

It can't be.

It's hopeless.

It's dark in here.

It's not a puzzle.

It's over.

It's really nothing at all.

It's so good to see you.

I've been here before.

I've never been so embarrassed in my life.

I've never flown so fast before.

Jump!

Just kidding.

Leave *now*.

Leave me alone.

Let's get out of here quick.

Let's get out of here.

Lint; it all comes down to lint.

Look out!

Look over there.

Never!

No way!

Oh, no!

Oh, yes!

Old age is not for sissies.

Ollie, ollie, oxen free.

Please don't make me.

Please say yes.

Please, no.

Quiet, they'll hear us.

Ready or not, here I come.

Red is my favorite color.

Ridiculous.

Run.

Ten, nine, eight …

Thanks so much.

That was the biggest chipmunk I've ever seen.

That's all I'm going to say about that.

First Line, Last Line

The phone's for you.

They're coming.

They're here.

This funnel should do the trick.

This has been the best day of my life.

This is all your fault.

This is not the end.

This is the end?

Trix are for kids.

Wait for me.

Watch out behind you.

Water!

We will.

We're trapped.

What are you doing here?

What did you say?

What?

What's in this box?

What's that crawling on your shoulder?

What's that noise?

What's that on your nose?

What's that?

What's wrong with you?

What's your problem?

When were you abducted by aliens?

Where?

Who turned off the lights?

Who's there?

Why did you do that?

Why did you make me do that?

Why don't you just leave?

Why, I never.

Wow, you look great today.

Yes?

You can't get rid of me that easily.

You did *what*?

You don't have to be a rocket scientist to understand this.

You don't know how long I've been waiting to hear you say that.

You don't look well.

You have a pet *what*?

You think you're so funny.

You think you're so smart.

You what?

SPACE PREP
5
MINUTES

PLAYER PREP
0
MINUTES

PERFORMANCE
5
MINUTES

Use These For:

Energy Expender

Group Skills

Icebreaker

Sponge

PLAYERS
2-4

Teach and Practice:

Blocking and Conventions

Characterization

Concentration

Creativity

Ensemble Acting

Following Directions

Group Dynamics

Listening and Silence

Memorization

Non-vocal Communication

Observation

Physical Control

Plot Structure

Spontaneity

EQUIPMENT
A table and 2-4 chairs.

Today's Your Lucky Day

Directions

- Divide into teams of two to four. Set up a table at a Chinese restaurant in the playing area.
- The players start the scene as diners at the end of the meal.
- The director gives one of the players a "fortune cookie" (a slip of paper or index card with a fortune).
- The player with the fortune reads the fortune to the players, and the scene progresses incorporating the fortune.

Examples

- *You will meet a tall, dark, handsome stranger.* The person with the fortune is about to leave the restaurant when the waiter recognizes her as an old girl-friend from high school whom he has been seeking for ten years.
- *Today is your lucky day.* The player with the fortune goes to pay the bill and finds out he is the restaurant's ten thousandth patron. He receives a voucher for ten free meals in the next year.

Evaluation/Critique

- How difficult was it for the players to incorporate the fortune into the scene?
- Did the fortune further the plot?
- Did the scene make sense?
- Was there a conclusive, logical ending to the scene?

Challenges and Refinements

- Other players may enter the scene.
- The players are given a fortune and have one minute to play a scene in which this fortune occurs.
- The director assigns the players *Characters* (page 85) or *Occupations* (page 105), and the players play the scene with those characters.

All your hair will fall out before tomorrow.

All your questions will be answered.

Always look on the bright side of life.

Are you sure you want to eat that?

Be generous to your waiter.

Be nice to your mother.

Be nice to your parents.

Beware of Chinese food.

Beware of killer bees.

Beware of people with tattoos.

Call your mother.

Check under your bed.

Check your safety deposit box.

Don't eat leftovers.

Don't look behind you.

Don't look in the mirror.

Don't marry the first person who comes around.

Don't pet strange dogs.

Don't do what the voices in your head tell you.

Don't drink that!

Don't leave the house on Tuesday.

Don't panic.

Duck!

Eat only Chinese food.

Everyone will know your name.

Expect the unexpected.

Fire danger extreme.

Life is a poisoned lollipop.

Look behind you!

Look both ways when crossing the street.

Never leave your house without sunscreen.

Never pick up a hitchhiker.

Never speak to men with peg legs.

Never speak to strangers.

Never take anything for granted.

Never wear blue.

Never wear the color red.

Put on a happy face.

Question authority.

Respect your elders.

Smile.

Stay away from electrical appliances for the next two weeks.

Stay away from people named Bob.

Stay home tomorrow.

Stop biting your fingernails.

That was not chicken.

The crickets you hear are not real.

Tomorrow is your lucky day.

Walk on the sunny side.

Watch where you step today.

Watch your step.

Why be normal?

Yesterday was your lucky day.

You are kind and generous.

You will choke on a fortune cookie.

You will discover that you have a superpower.

You will discover the cure for cancer.

You will discover the meaning of life.

You will find a hidden treasure.

You will gain 100 pounds in the next five years.

You will gain fame and fortune.

You will get accepted to the college of your choice.

You will go on a long journey.

You will have a terrible accident but will recover from it.

You will have three successful children.

You will inherit a million dollars.

You will lead a long and prosperous life.

You will learn an important lesson.

You will make a great discovery.

You will marry a millionaire.

You will marry royalty.

You will meet a tall, dark stranger.

You will move to a different state.

You will narrowly escape death.

You will receive an important phone call.

You will receive good news.

You will take a journey over water.

You will win a prestigious award.

You will win the lottery.

You will win the Nobel Peace Prize.

Your book will finally get published.

Your dog will become infested with fleas.

Your future could look brighter.

Your future looks bright.

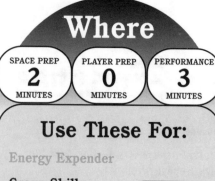

SPACE PREP
2
MINUTES

PLAYER PREP
0
MINUTES

PERFORMANCE
3
MINUTES

Use These For:

Energy Expender

Group Skills

Icebreaker

Sponge

PLAYERS
5-6

Teach and Practice:

Blocking and Conventions

Characterization

Concentration

Creativity

Ensemble Acting

Following Directions

Group Dynamics

Listening and Silence

Memorization

Non-vocal Communication

Observation

Physical Control

Plot Structure

Spontaneity

EQUIPMENT
5 or 6 chairs or a bench.

Freeze

Directions

- Divide into teams of five to six. Players sit on a bench or chairs in front of the group.
- The director assigns a scenario that the players start immediately.
- As the first scene progresses, the director calls out, *"One, two, three — Freeze."*
- At freeze, the players freeze as if they were caught in a photo of the scene.
- The director continues by calling, *"unfreeze,"* and giving the players a new scene.

Examples

- Choose a place such as a movie theatre.
- Call out the scene in chronological order so that characters and relationships can develop.

Side Coaching (for Movie Theatre)

- Use your entire body!
- Remember levels, spacing, and facial expressions!
- React to the movie!
- React to your fellow moviegoers!

Evaluation/Critique (for Movie Theatre)

- Were the frozen pictures visually interesting?
- Did the pictures tell a story?
- Were the characters reacting to each other?
- Was there a focus on the screen, or was the focus split?
- What characters caught your attention? Why?

Challenges and Refinements

- Try this game as a focus game. During the freeze, call out the name of one of the players and ask them to take focus. Ask the other players to give focus.
- Develop one of the freezes into a scene.

Freeze Scenarios

File name on CD: FrzScen

At the movie theatre

You smell something.

The smell is coming from you.

The smell is coming from the person next to you.

You snuck in, and an usher is checking tickets.

Your girlfriend/boyfriend is three rows ahead with another date.

You are in an R-rated movie, and you are only thirteen.

The film broke.

The movie is very violent.

The movie is very sad.

The movie is very confusing.

The movie is very funny.

The movie is very suspenseful.

It's extremely bloody, and blood makes you throw up.

Someone spilled buttered popcorn on you.

You stepped in gum.

You have to go to the bathroom, but you just can't leave.

Two people are necking in front of you.

Two people are talking behind you.

In the doctor's office

You have been waiting for two hours.

You have read all the magazines.

A person who got there after you is called in.

The doctor brings you good news.

The doctor brings you bad news.

You find out you need a painful shot.

The call to the principal's office

The other kids there are notorious troublemakers.

You have never — *ever* — gotten into trouble in school before.

You wonder if they found that "thing" in your locker.

Your parents walk in.

The principal looks extremely grim.

The principal has a big smile.

The principal shakes your hand.

At the rock concert

At the opera

At the beauty pageant

At the dog show

At the hair salon

SPACE PREP	PLAYER PREP	PERFORMANCE
2	**0**	**5**
MINUTES	MINUTES	MINUTES

Use These For:

Energy Expender

Group Skills

Icebreaker

Sponge

PLAYERS
2-4

Teach and Practice:

Blocking and Conventions

Characterization

Concentration

Creativity

Ensemble Acting

Following Directions

Group Dynamics

Listening and Silence

Memorization

Non-vocal Communication

Observation

Physical Control

Plot Structure

Spontaneity

EQUIPMENT
Assorted tables, chairs, and props as available and needed.

In the Style Of

Directions

- Divide into teams of two to four.
- The audience chooses a title or generic scene for the players to improvise.
- Players start the scene in the present (twenty-first century).
- As the scene progresses, the director calls out a new time period (see *Time Periods*, page 157), and the players gradually shift to a new period and its requisite "style."

Side Coaching

- Make the switch believable!
- Keep your same personality characteristics, but modify them to suit the time period!

Example

The first date. The action starts in the twenty-first century with the couple having their photos taken by the proud parents in the girl's living room. They switch to the eighteenth century where the couple is posing for a portrait painter. They then switch to the stone age where the parents are painting the picture on a cave wall.

Evaluation/Critique

- Did the time changes seem believable?
- Were the transitions smooth?
- Are the original characters still recognizable?

Challenges and Refinements

- Divide the large group into teams of two to four.
- Give each team a different time period.
- The entire group shows the same scene in different time periods.

For more prompts, try *Film Titles* (page 61) and *Clichés* (page 29).

Generic Scenes

File name on CD: GScenes

a visit to a foreign country where you don't speak the language

alien invasion

armed robbery

at a car wash

at a funeral

at the fat farm

at the movies

audition

awards ceremony

bank robbery

beauty pageant

being bullied

being the new kid in school

blind date

breaking up

car accident

car chase

caught in a tourist trap

cheating on a test

cleaning the closet

court appearance

driving test

execution

facelift

family reunion

family vacation

first airplane trip

first baby

first dance

first date

first day at summer camp

first day at yoga class

first day in the Army

first day of kindergarten

first day of school

first day on the job

first day teaching

getting a manicure or facial

getting to know you

graduation

in detention

job interview

locked in

lost at the mall

lost in a maze

lost in the woods

marriage proposal

meet the parents

moving

new puppy

on the roller coaster

passing notes in class

picking pockets

prison escape

prisoner of war camp

purchasing a new home

roommates

senior prom

shoplifting

surgery

taking a test

talent contest

trapped

trip to the zoo

tunnel of love

visit to the dentist

visit to the hospital

How

SPACE PREP
2
MINUTES

PLAYER PREP
5
MINUTES

PERFORMANCE
3
MINUTES

Use These For:

Energy Expender

Group Skills

PLAYERS
3-5

Icebreaker

Sponge

Teach and Practice:

Blocking and Conventions

Characterization

Concentration

Creativity

Ensemble Acting

Following Directions

Group Dynamics

Listening and Silence

Memorization

Non-vocal Communication

Observation

Physical Control

Plot Structure

Spontaneity

EQUIPMENT
Assorted tables, chairs, and props as available and needed.

In This Genre

Directions

- Divide into teams of three to five.
- Each team draws or is assigned the title of a film (see *Film Titles* on page 61 with titles such as, *The People Next Door, The Red Door, The Closet*, etc., or the American Film Institute's top 100 films).
- The teams are each given a genre (adventure, children's show, science fiction, etc.) and must develop this title as if it were a classic example of this film genre.
- The teams develop episodes of a film or TV show that illustrates the title in their genres. (They may use lists of appropriate *Genre Jogs* [page 75] to provide ideas.)

Side Coaching

- Use the genre jogs to get ideas for plot and characterization!
- Be sure your scene has at least one conflict!
- Be sure that conflicts are resolved!
- Be sure you have a beginning, middle, and an end!

Example

- *The People Next Door* as a horror movie.
- *The Red Door* as a children's show.
- *The Closet* as a documentary.

Evaluation/Critique

- Was the scene true to the title?
- Was the scene true to the genre?
- What aspects of the genre were emphasized?

●com American Film Institute
www.afi.com

Genres

action/adventure

biography

children

comedy

cooking

crime/mystery

disaster

documentary

Elizabethan

fairy tales

fantasy

historical

home improvement

horror

infomercials

law

medical

musicals

mythology

nature

news

opera

quiz

romance

science fiction

soap opera

talk show

teen

western

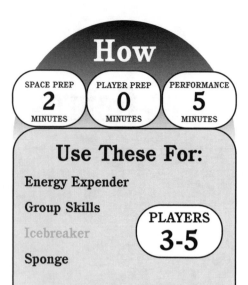

SPACE PREP	PLAYER PREP	PERFORMANCE
2 MINUTES	**0** MINUTES	**5** MINUTES

Use These For:

Energy Expender

Group Skills

Icebreaker

Sponge

PLAYERS 3-5

Teach and Practice:

Blocking and Conventions

Characterization

Concentration

Creativity

Ensemble Acting

Following Directions

Group Dynamics

Listening and Silence

Memorization

Non-vocal Communication

Observation

Physical Control

Plot Structure

Spontaneity

EQUIPMENT
5 chairs; optional desk.
Optional — tape to mark
playing areas.

Genre House

Directions

- Divide into teams of three to five.
- Divide the playing area into four equal sections. The group decides what genre will be performed in each section.
- The group or director gives a title for a scene that reflects the starting genre. (*Film Titles* on page 61 and *Clichés* on page 29 offer good titles.)
- The players start a scene in the first genre, establishing who, when, and where.
- The director calls, "switch," and the players move to a new area/genre and continue the scene in the new genre.

Side Coaching

- Use jogs to help develop scenes in each genre!
- Make the transition between genres clear!
- Gradually switch into the new genre!

Example

The stage is divided into *horror, soap opera, news broadcast,* and *children's show*. The scene title is, "The People Next Door." The players start in *children's show* with one player as a parent explaining to the other player, a child, about the new people who moved in next door and how nice it will be to have new friends.

At the switch they move into *soap opera* in which the child is terribly upset and tells the parent about an exaggerated situation going on next door. At the next switch, they move to *horror* in which they discover the dead bodies of the new neighbors. At the final switch they are interviewed live at the scene of the crime.

Options

- The director may elect to let the players choose where to start and finish, *or* the director may call out the genre areas when it is time to switch.
- The players are given a list of words from each genre, which they may use to help their scene.

The list of *Genre Jogs* on the CD-ROM has a unique format.

Action/Adventure

aircraft
analysis
Army Rangers
assassination
betrayal
bizarre
bomb
buddy
car chase
clue
code
conspirator
dagger
decontamination
detonate
disarm
drug deal
elude
engineer
epidemic
extortion
fraud
garrote
guilt
headset
helicopter
hideout
high explosives (HE)
high speed
homicide
Humvee
intelligence/intel
intuition
invade
investigation
jet
kiss
knife
lie detector
machine gun
macho
Marine

mercenary
National Security Council
nerves
passion
pathogen
perpetrator
poison
poison gas
problem
radiation
rockets
safe house
SCUBA
Seal Team
security
seizure
sidearm
sidekick
silencer
static
subdued
submarine
suspicion
top secret
torpedo
toxin
transmission
truth serum
Uzi
victim
VTOL
warfare
weapon

Biography

accounts
accurate
adventure
alive
betrayal
bitter
conspirator
depression

discreet
doubt
early indications
education
envy
estate
faith
fame
guilt
hang
hero
heroic
honorable
hope
humble beginnings
illegitimate
inherited
intelligent
invade
jealousy
legacy
marriage
minister
newspaper
nobility
notoriety
obstacle
overcome
parents
postmortem
precocious
pride
priest
prodigy
quintessential
reliable source
religion
report
responsible
sources
subdued
success
teachers

truth
values

Children

alphabet
arithmetic
brother
caring
cartoon
choices
chore
coloring book
count
crayons
dreams
effort
exciting
fabulous
fantastic
father
fear
fever
friends
funny
good guys
romantic comedy
running gag
satire
sentimental
sharp
shtick
shy
sight gag
silent film
sitcom
sketch
skit
spoof
stand up
story
storytelling
style
taut

Genre Jogs

tender
time step
time-defying
timing
tolerance
tone
uncompromising
understatement
unexpected
unique
unpredictable
versatile
virtuosity
vivid
writers

Cooking

asparagus
bake
baking powder
baking soda
beat
beer
blend
boil
braise
bread
briskly
broil
celery
chocolate
choice
combine
cream
deep-fry
dough
eggs
endive
flour
fold
frappé
fresh
frozen

fry
garnish
greens
highest quality
home cooking
ice
ingredients
juice
lettuce
measure carefully
milk
mix
oil
okra
olive oil
olives
onions
paté
pears
peas
pepper
presentation
prime
purest ingredients
rice
salt
sauce
sauté
season
shortcut
slowly
smell
soufflé
stir
sugar
taste
test with a toothpick
truffles
undercooked
vanilla
vegetables
vinegar
watermelon

whip
wine
yeast

Crime/Mystery

10-4
bond
bounty
buddy
burglar
butler
camera
car chase
cat burglar
code
communications
computer
confession
constable
contaminated
criminology
culpable
danger
detective
disarm
district attorney
drown
drug deal
elude
evaluation
evidence
evil
ex-con
experiment
extortion
felon
felony
forensics
fraud
garrote
guilt
hang
helicopter

hideout
high speed
homicide
inebriated
intelligence
investigation
jail
knife
laboratory
lead pipe
lie detector
manslaughter
melodramatic
missing person
mugger
neglect
perpetrator
pistol
poison
police
post mortem
prison
red herring
report
responsible
rigor mortis
security
sidearm
silencer
strangle
suicide
suspect
suspicion
unidentified body
victim
wanted
weapon

Disaster

airplane crash
anxiety
blizzard
bravery

cauldron
collapse
conflagration
death toll
devastation
dire
earthquake
escape
evacuate
evacuation
eventful
explode
fear
fire
firestorm
flood
heroism
hinder
horror
illness
inferno
landslide
martial law
panic
rescue
Richter scale
riot
salvage
shipwreck
sinister
sink
teamwork
temblor
terror
thwart
volcano

Documentary
air power
airspace
alcoholic
anthropologist
astronaut

atomic bomb
biochemist
bomb
bury
camera
Civil War
conspiracy
debacle
Desert Storm
detonate
drug deal
Earth
epidemic
evidence
experiment
expose
exposé
facts
fighter plane
flying ace
genetics
gravity
helicopter
heroic
historical
hope
horse
infectious
invasion
jet
Korea
laboratory
little-known
meteor
Middle East
missing person
national security
navigation
neglect
newspaper
physics
plague
presidential power

Prohibition
radar
radiation
reconnaissance
report
research
rocket
Russia
SCUBA
security
shadow of doubt
sidearm
silence
Sopwith Camel
space program
submarine
technology
The Great Depression
The Great War/World
　War I
Titanic
top secret
transmission
tsunami
USSR
Vietnam
warfare
World War II

Elizabethan
actor
betwixt
bodkin
boy company
comedy
doth
groundling
history
methinks
perchance
Queen
quoth
'tis

tragedy
'twas
twixt
varlet
villain

Fairy Tales/Fantasy
amulet
changeling
charm
demon
destiny
dwarf
elf
enchanter
evil spirit
fairy
fate
goblin
happily ever after
heaven
hero
incantation
magic
magic carpet
monster
omen
once upon a time
oracle
orc
prince
princess
quest
riddle
ring
rune
sacrifice
spell
test
warlock
witch
wizard

Genre Jogs

Historical
alive
amateur
asphyxiate
autopsy
betrayal
bitter
bounty
brute
bury
conspiracy
conspirator
constable
culpable
debacle
depression
doubt
drown
envy
estate
faith
fear
felony
fever
fraud
guilt
hang
homicide
hope
illegitimate
inherited
insurance
invade
jealousy
legacy
lust
neglect
poison gas
pride
problem
professional
reaction
report
responsible
revenge
security
soothe
spat
strangle
subdued
suicide
suspect
trust
truth
uncompromising
wanted
widow

Home Improvement
architect
attic
blinds
Bob Vila
brick
ceiling
chimney
chisel
circuit box
concrete
contractor
crawl space
curtains
cut
door
drapery
drill
dry rot
dry wall
electricity
entry
exhaust
fixtures
footings
frame
framing square
hardware
hardwood
hinge
joist
lighting
mantle
mastic
millwork
miter box
moldings
nail
old house
pipe chase
plaster
plumb
plumbing
refinishing
screw gun
screwdriver
shower
shutters
siding
stud
tile
vanity
wallboard
wallpaper
window

Horror
stealth
strangle
subdued
suspect
suspense
toxin
transmission
transplant
undead
vampire
vein
virus
voodoo
werewolf
zombie

Infomercial
$19.95
_____ of the stars
amazing
applause
authentic
bonus offer
charming
easy
entertaining
enthusiasm
exaggeration
free shipping
George Foreman
Ginsu Knives
hype
incredible
limited edition
limited quantities
limited-time offer
money-back guarantee
one-time offer
only five left
opportunity
Ronco
sales pitch
savings
set it and forget it
simple
spectacular
testimonial
vintage

Law
alimony
animosity
bar exam
beneficiary
bequeath
betrayal
billing
brief

briefing
children's court
children's court judge
civil case
computer
conspiracy
conspirator
court reporter
criminal case
crisis
defendant
discreet
district attorney
district court
divorce
drug deal
evaluation
evidence
exhibit
expert witness
facts
felony
fraud
gag order
guilt
homicide
inherited
instrument
insurance
intuition
judge
jury
justice of the peace (J.P.)
law clerk
law school
magistrate court
manipulation
melodrama
melodramatic
municipal court
paralegal
penitentiary
plaintiff

police chief
problem
procedure
professional
report
scam
security
seizure
silence
Supreme Court
suspect
tort
trust
truth
witness

Medical
amoebic dysentery
artery
bacteria
biological warfare
blood pressure
brain function
cadaver
cancer
cardiologist
chaplain
clinic
coma
contaminated
convulsion
crisis
depression
diet
disinfectant
drug-induced
emergency vehicle
epidemic
evaluation
experiment
facts
fever
forensics

fracture
gloves
gown
heart attack
hypertension
hypochondria
hypothermia
infectious
instrument
insurance
intern
intravenous
laboratory
mask
med student
medication
microscope
nausea
neurosis
nutritionist
operating room (O.R.)
oncologist
oscilloscope
paralyzed
paraplegic
pathogen
pharmacy
phobia
physician
pills
procedure
professional
psychosomatic
psychotic
radiation
reaction
report
research
resident
respiration
scalpel
seizure
stat

sterile
steroids
toxin
tranquilizer
transmission
transplant
uniform
vein
virus

Musicals
act
ballad
baritone
bass
beat
Broadway
character actor
choreographer
choreography
chorus
chorus line
chorus number
color
comedy
conductor
contralto
costume designer
dance
dance captain
dialogue coach
director
downbeat
drama
duet
emotion
finale
happily ever after
ingénue
juvenile
kick line
lead
librettist

Genre Jogs

libretto
love
orchestra
orchestra pit
patter song
plot
romance
scene
score
sing
solo
song
soprano
special effect
tap dancers
tempo
tenor
Tin Pan Alley
up-tempo

Mythology
alive
Atlantis
banshee
basilisk
battle
Centaur
conquest
creation
destiny
dragon
dwarf
elf
envy
epic
evil spirit
faith
fate
flood
flying horse/Pegasus
folk tale
giant
god

Gorgon
griffin
guilt
Hades
harpy
heaven
hero
heroine
honesty
hope
hubris
immortality
incantation
infant
invade
jealousy
legend
Lernean Hydra
Leviathan
love
lust
magic
Midgard Serpent
Minotaur
miracle
monster
mystery
Nemean Lion
Odyssey
ogre
patricide
phoenix
quest
revenge
riddle
robber
rune
sacrifice
satyr
scream
sea serpent
self-sacrifice
Siren

soothsayer
Sphinx
strangle
suicide
superpowers
test
troll
truth
uncompromising
wonder

Nature
Africa
Amazon
Australia
crocodiles
danger
exploitation
extinction
hunters
instructive
monsters
photographers
predator
risk
sharks
snakes
tourists
vicious

News
anchor
assistant
background
breaking story
broadcast
crime
desk
exposé
human interest
lifestyle
meteorologist
news flash

politics
reporter
sound byte
sports
sportscaster
talent
top story
tragedy
weather
weather person

Opera
coloratura
comedy
conductor
contralto
drama
emotion
German
Italian
libretto
mezzo-soprano
Mozart
prompter
recitative
score
soprano
tenor
vibrato

Quiz
answer
buy
choose
door number three
free
host
level
lost
luck
money
next level
prize

question
select
selection
sell
spin
spokesmodel
supermodel
time
won

Romance/Romantic Comedy
anxious
argument
best man
boyfriend
bride
buddy
confusion
envy
friend
girlfriend
groom
husband
jealousy
kiss
love
lover
maid of honor
make up
misunderstanding
mixup
passion
quarrel
sex
spat
wife

Science Fiction
air lock
airspace
airwaves
alien

amoeba
analysis
android
animosity
anthropologist
artery
asphyxiate
asteroid
atmosphere
audio
automaton
autopsy
biological warfare
biology
biophysicist
black hole
blood pressure
brain function
briefing
camouflage
captain's log
chemical warfare
code
comet
commander
communications
computer
conspiracy
conspirator
constellation
contaminated
covert
crisis
cyborg
death
death star
decontamination
deep space
detonate
disinfectant
diversion
earphone
Earthling

eclipse
emergency
emergency vehicle
engineer
epidemic
ether
evaluation
experiment
extraterrestrial
facts
formation
gaseous
genetics
gravity
helicopter
hypothermia
infectious
inhuman
instrument
intelligence
intuition
invade
invisibility
laboratory
landing site
lift off
meteor
microscope
mind control
moon
mother ship
navigation
nebula
nerves
nonliving
nova
oscilloscope
oxygen
pathogen
phobia
physicist
plague
planet

poison gas
radar
reaction
report
research
robot
rocket
satellite
scientist
seizure
sky
slime
solar system
spaceship
space station
spaceport
star
starship trooper
static
sterile
storm trooper
sub ether
submarine
sun
technology
telescope
toxin
tranquilizer
transplant
transporter
turmoil
universe
vacuum
virus
wormhole
wrinkle in time

Soap Opera
affair
alcoholic
alimony
amnesia
anguish

Genre Jogs

animosity
betrayal
bigamy
bizarre
cancer
cheat
children
coma
confession
depression
diet
discreet
divorce
drug addict
drug-induced
duplicity
envy
evidence
exhibitionist
facts
forgiveness
fraud
friendless
fury
greed
guilt
heart
heart attack
home wrecker
hypochondria
illegitimate
inebriated
infidelity
inherited
insurance
jealousy
legacy
libel
loathing
lust
manipulation
mediation
melodramatic

missing person
neurosis
orphan
other woman
passion
penitentiary
phobia
post mortem
pregnant
pride
psychosomatic
psychotic
revenge
rumor
sarcasm
scandal
scorn
scream
seizure
slander
smother
spiteful
steroids
strangle
suicide
sulk
suspect
swindle

Talk Show
abandon
addict
alcoholic
aliens
amnesia
anorexia
Betty Ford
bigamy
bizarre
book tour
Botox
brain research
bulimia

bungee jumper
celebrity
coma
commercial
cosmetic surgery
deadbeat
degrade
desperate
diet plan (latest)
dish the dirt
drunk driver
dysfunctional
emotion
environmentalist
exercise program
exhibitionist
experiment
fantasy
fat transplant
fatal disease
feelings
fight
gender
grooming
hair
host
humiliate
kiss-and-tell
knife
latest movie
lawsuit
liposuction
makeover
model
molest
Mommy Dearest
motorcycle gang
obese
obsession
penitentiary
phenomenon
piercing
poignant

psychiatrist
pumping iron
revenge
rollerblade
sensuality
spandex
survival
tattoo
tears
tell-all
therapy
torment
tranquilizer
transplant
transsexual
transvestite
vegetarian
violent
zoo animals

Teen
auto shop
backpack
band
baseball
beauty
beer
boyfriend
car crash
cell (phone)
cheat
cheerleader
choir
clothes
college
compete
contraception
crazy
creep
dance
dancer
drag race
drama

drink
drive
drive-in
drugs
drunk
envy
exams
fear
football
frighten
gang
girlfriend
hair
hang (out)
hate
high school
history
homework
hot
incurable disease
jealousy
kiss
math
mobile (phone)
mother
parents
party
performing arts
phone
poetry
rock
rock and roll
roommate
science
sex
shoes
sister
social studies
sock hop
spite
teacher
team
truck
urban legend

Western

ambush
bandit
beans
bounty hunter
bow and arrow
box canyon
branding iron
buffalo
bunkhouse
cactus
canyon
cattle drive
chuckwagon
corral
cowpoke
coyote
dance hall girl
deputy
desert
desert rat
desperado
dogie
donkey
dust storm
farmer
flash flood
foothill
gambling
ghost town
gold mine
gold pan
gold rush
grazing
grubstake
gunfight
high noon
hitching post
holdup
Indian
lynch
marshal
mountain
mountain lion

mule
neck rag
outlaw
oxen
pioneer
posse
prospector
railroad
ranch
rifle
saddle blanket
sagebrush
saloon
schoolmarm
scout
settler
sheriff
shootout
shotgun
sidekick
six-shooter
spread
spurs
stagecoach
steak
strongbox
trail
wagon train
water hole
watering trough
well
windmill

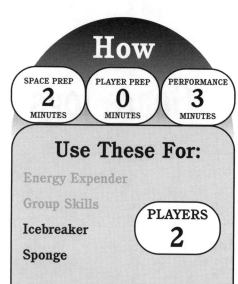

How

SPACE PREP	PLAYER PREP	PERFORMANCE
2	**0**	**3**
MINUTES	MINUTES	MINUTES

Use These For:

Energy Expender

Group Skills

PLAYERS
2

Icebreaker

Sponge

Teach and Practice:

Blocking and Conventions

Characterization

Concentration

Creativity

Ensemble Acting

Following Directions

Group Dynamics

Listening and Silence

Memorization

Non-vocal Communication

Observation

Physical Control

Plot Structure

Spontaneity

EQUIPMENT

2 chairs and a desk.

News Commentary

Directions

- Divide into teams of two. Pairs of players are chosen to anchor a news broadcast.
- The director selects a headline from the list.
- The players present the "news" in the style of _____ (use *Characters* or *Literary Styles on page 85*).
- The director changes style with every new headline as the anchors switch off.

Examples

- *Bat Boy Escapes from Prison* in the style of a scared little kid.
- *Fat Men Make Better Boyfriends* in the style of a revenge tragedy.

Side Coaching

- Don't worry if the style doesn't seem to fit the topic!
- Keep up the pace!
- Elaborate on the story!

Evaluation/Critique

- Did the anchors seem serious?
- Were the stories fleshed out with details?
- Did the anchors' voices and body language fit the styles?

Challenges and Refinements

- Switch styles in the middle of an anchor's story.
- Add extra players to go "on the scene" and act out the headline.
- Make a full-fledged news broadcast using several headlines and different styles.

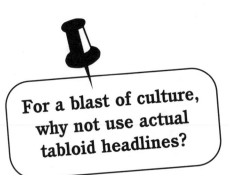

For a blast of culture, why not use actual tabloid headlines?

News Commentary Ideas

Headlines

200-pound baby born
500-pound man leaves house
Aliens invade Earth
Angels reveal themselves
Bat boy escapes from prison
Bigfoot wedding
Butterflies carry fatal disease
Child born with purple eyes
Christmas lights hazardous to health
Color pink can make you rich
Dog-worshipping religion spreads
Dracula escapes
Elvis weds alien
Fat men make better boyfriends
Giant spider on the loose
Immortality imminent
Invasion from Mars
Kissing causes cancer
Landfills source of cancer cure
Lock Ness Monster discovered
   in Japan
Luxembourg invades Pakistan
Mad scientist invents super weapon
Miracle food discovered
Miss Cleo reveals all
Nobel Prize awarded to child
Rabid dog attacks kindergarten class
Race of one-inch-high people
   discovered in Florida
Stephen King wins Pulitzer Prize
Tattooing good for health
Ten-year-old buys winning lottery
   ticket
Terror on the tramway
Tribe of orange-skinned pygmies
   found
Two-headed baby born

Characters

911 operator
alcoholic
ballet instructor
cheerleader
clown
cop
cowboy
Crocodile Hunter
detective
fearful person
film critic
football coach
French waiter
Hollywood starlet
kindergarten teacher
librarian
Mafia Don
motivational speaker
multiple personality person
news broadcaster
old-time preacher
opera singer
paranoid person
person speaking in tongues
phone friend
priest
psychiatrist
psychic
punk rocker
realtor
redneck
salesperson
scared little kid
Shakespearean actor
sportscaster
stand-up comic
student body president
superhero
telephone solicitor
vampire
whiny brat
Woody Allen

Literary Styles

File name on CD: LitStyles

Agatha Christie
chick lit
child's letter to Grandma
Dick and Jane
Dickens
Dr. Seuss
Edgar Allen Poe
e-mail message
erotica
forties noir
gothic novel
haiku
Hemingway
horror
inspirational
Jane Austen
limerick
love letter
mythology
New Testament
New York Times editorial
Old Testament
recipe
revenge tragedy
romantic fiction
romantic poetry
Shakespeare
Sherlock Holmes
sonnet
tabloid article
textbook
theatre of the absurd
travel writing
women's magazine fiction

When

SPACE PREP	PLAYER PREP	PERFORMANCE
2	**5**	**2**
MINUTES	MINUTES	MINUTES

Use These For:

Energy Expender

Group Skills

Icebreaker

**PLAYERS
4-6**

Sponge

Teach and Practice:

Blocking and Conventions

Characterization

Concentration

Creativity

Ensemble Acting

Following Directions

Group Dynamics

Listening and Silence

Memorization

Non-vocal Communication

Observation

Physical Control

Plot Structure

Spontaneity

EQUIPMENT

Optional: levels, benches, stools.

Wax Museum

Directions

- Divide into teams of four to six.
- Each team thinks of, draws, or is assigned a historical moment. (See also *Past Times* on page 113 and *Time Periods* on page 157.)
- Teams develop three to five "pictures" representing aspects of that moment.
- When finished, teams perform for each other. Frozen scenes should be performed in chronological order.

Examples

Jack the Ripper Stalks London.

1. People crowd around a newspaper and react in horror.
2. Police search the streets.
3. Jack lures a prostitute.
4. Jack dismembers his victim.
5. Policeman discovers the body.

Side Coaching

- Don't forget to use gestures, levels, and facial and body expressions!
- Strive for variety of mood!
- Tell a story!
- Stick to chronological order!

Evaluation/Critique

- Was the historical moment clear?
- Were the aspects of the moment building on each other?
- Did the pictures tell a story?
- Were the pictures visually interesting?

Historical Moments

File name on CD: HistMoments

Crimes
Jack the Ripper stalks London
Oklahoma City Bombing

Disasters
Black Plague
Chicago Fire (1871)
Chernobyl Nuclear Disaster
Hindenburg explodes
San Francisco earthquake (1906)
Sinking of the Titanic
Three Mile Island

Discoveries
King Tut's tomb opened
Lewis and Clark arrive at the Pacific
Mayflower lands at Plymouth Rock
Neil Armstrong steps onto the moon
Russians orbit Sputnik

Economy
The Great Depression
Stock Market Crash in 1929

Heroism
Flag planted at Iwo Jima
Joan of Arc fights the British
The Underground Railroad

Invention
Alexander Graham Bell invents the telephone
Gutenberg invents movable type
Henry Ford builds the Model A

Law
Napoleonic Code written
Signing of the Declaration of Independence
Signing of the Magna Carta

Literature
Shakespeare writes his first play

Music
Beatles perform on Ed Sullivan Show

Politics
Cuban Missile Crisis
Fall of Berlin Wall
Gandhi kicks the Brits out of India
Guillotine used in French Revolution
Julius Caesar assassinated
Lincoln gives the Gettysburg Address
Socrates drinks hemlock
U.S. buys Alaska from Russia
Watergate

Progress
Golden spike laid at Promontory Point

Science
Archimedes says, "Eureka"
The Curies discover radioactivity
Darwin visits the Galapagos
First successful heart transplant
Galileo says Earth rotates around sun
Polio vaccine perfected

War
9-11
The Alamo
Battle of Waterloo
Boston Tea Party
Custer's Last Stand
Hannibal crosses the Alps
Pearl Harbor
Lusitania
Trojan War

Who

SPACE PREP
0
MINUTES

PLAYER PREP
0
MINUTES

PERFORMANCE
~
MINUTES

Use These For:

Energy Expender

Group Skills

Icebreaker

Sponge

PLAYERS
2

Teach and Practice:

Blocking and Conventions

Characterization

Concentration

Creativity

Ensemble Acting

Following Directions

Group Dynamics

Listening and Silence

Memorization

Non-vocal Communication

Observation

Physical Control

Plot Structure

Spontaneity

EQUIPMENT
Optional: chairs, benches, levels, stools.

Sick

Directions

- Divide into teams of two.
- Each player draws an illness.
- Without knowing the illnesses, the audience chooses a situation, relationship, generic scene, or title for the scene. (*Film Titles* page 61, *Generic Scenes* page 71, *Status Relationships* page 151.)
- Players improvise a scene in which each character has an illness. The type of illness determines the plot.

Example

First Date: The male has chicken pox and the female has a nervous disorder. He takes her to a restaurant where his constant itching drives her to a nervous breakdown.

Side Coaching

- Show your illness!
- Let your illness drive the plot!

Evaluation/Critique

- What physical or mental manifestations of the illness were shown?
- Did the players use all their senses?
- Which senses were used most frequently?

Challenges and Refinements

The Creeping Crud
- Start with selecting illness and situation as before.
- Players begin in good health, but as the scene progresses so do their illnesses.

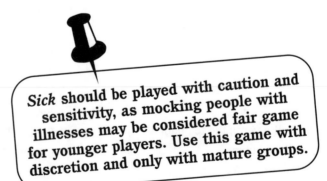

Sick should be played with caution and sensitivity, as mocking people with illnesses may be considered fair game for younger players. Use this game with discretion and only with mature groups.

acid reflux disease

acne

ADHD

agoraphobia

AIDS

alcoholism

Alzheimer's

arachnophobia

asthma

astigmatism

autism

beriberi

bipolar disorder

blindness

broken arm

broken collarbone

broken elbow

broken leg

cancer

carpal tunnel syndrome

cerebral palsy

chicken pox

cholera

claustrophobia

cold

deafness

depression

diabetes

dysentery

earache

farsightedness

fear of heights

gingivitis

hangnails

hantavirus

headache

heart disease

high blood pressure

high cholesterol

hysteria

ingrown toenails

Lyme disease

macular degeneration

mad cow disease

mania

measles

meningitis

migraine

multiple personality disorder

multiple sclerosis

mumps

narcissism

nearsightedness

nervous disorder

obsessive-compulsive disorder

oppositional disorder

paranoia

respiratory disease

Rocky Mountain spotted fever

rubella

SARS

schizophrenia

sinus infection

sleeping sickness

slipped disc

smallpox

TMJ

toothache

torn Achilles tendon

torn ACL

Tourette syndrome

tuberculosis

typhoid fever

vertigo

West Nile virus

whooping cough

yellow fever

SPACE PREP
2
MINUTES

PLAYER PREP
0
MINUTES

PERFORMANCE
5
MINUTES

Use These For:

Energy Expender

Group Skills

Icebreaker

Sponge

PLAYERS
3-7

Teach and Practice:

Blocking and Conventions

Characterization

Concentration

Creativity

Ensemble Acting

Following Directions

Group Dynamics

Listening and Silence

Memorization

Non-vocal Communication

Observation

Physical Control

Plot Structure

Spontaneity

EQUIPMENT
Benches or stools.

Twisted

Directions

- Divide into teams of three to seven. One player sits in the playing area at the far end of a bench. Up to six players line up outside the playing area.
- One at a time, players from the team enter the scene and create an improbable physical trait for the seated player.
- The seated player (player 1) accepts the newcomer's (player 2) lead as to the where, when, why, and who of the scene, all the time trying to discover his or her unusual physical trait within the confines of the scene.
- When the seated player guesses what the trait is, he or she immediately assumes it and finds a motivation for exiting.
- Player 1 goes to the back of the line, and player 2 sits on the bench.
- Play continues with the next player in line.

Example

Second player enters as a policeman and starts grilling the seated player about a recent robbery. By suggestion, he endows the seated player with *wheels for legs*, which explains how the player escaped the scene of the crime so quickly. The seated player realizes that the cop is onto him and wheels away.

Side Coaching

- Show! Don't tell!
- As soon as you guess your trait, get physical!
- Use your trait for movement (example — huge feet would make it difficult to walk gracefully)!
- Show your trait!
- Act as if the other player already knows. Let your hints be part of your normal reaction to his/her trait!

Evaluation/Critique

- What kinds of interaction helped the seated player to guess his trait?
- How did the second player suggest the trait without giving it away?
- How did the trait influence the plot?
- How did the trait influence the way the second player interacted with the seated one?

Improbable Physical Traits

File name on CD: IPT

a bark for a voice

a square head

a tail

a voice like a growl

a white streak down the middle of black hair

arm in the abdomen

bad body odor

badly bitten nails

bent in half

bumps all over the body

claws for hands

constantly fidgeting

crooked smile

drooping ear lobes

Dumbo ears

extremely short

extremely tall

eyes in the back of the head

greasy hair

green skin

head on backwards

hole in the head

huge eyes

huge jowls

huge mouth

inflated cheeks like a chipmunk

large overbite

long fingernails

long toenails that stick out of the shoes

long, long hair

missing arms

missing legs

no elbows

no knees

no nose

one finger on each hand

one short leg/one long leg

peg leg

pink hair

revolving neck

scales on the skin

six double chins

six fingers on each hand

six-inch legs with large feet

size 20 shoes

sloshes when moves

smiles all the time

tentacles for arms

three eyes

three legs

tiny feet

twisted like a pretzel

two heads

very long nose

wears six-inch heels

weighs 600 pounds

wheels for feet

withered hands

woman with a beard

Use These For:

Energy Expender

Group Skills

Icebreaker

Sponge

PLAYERS
Full Group

Teach and Practice:

Blocking and Conventions

Characterization

Concentration

Creativity

Ensemble Acting

Following Directions

Group Dynamics

Listening and Silence

Memorization

Non-vocal Communication

Observation

Physical Control

Plot Structure

Spontaneity

EQUIPMENT
None.

SPACE PREP
0
MINUTES

PLAYER PREP
0
MINUTES

PERFORMANCE
~
MINUTES

Line at a Time

Directions

- Players form two equal lines facing each other.
- One at a time, a player from each side goes to the center and says a line for one of the topics called by the director.
- "Passing" is not an option. Players must say something, clever or not.
- Topics change whenever the director feels the energy ebbing.

Examples

- For *horror movie titles:*
  - The Thing That Ate My Teacher
  - The Neighbor's Pet
  - Tasty Toes
- For *excuses for being late to class:*
  - My locker jammed.
  - A ten-foot monster attacked me.
  - I was called to the principal's office.

(Notice the switch from realism to fantasy. Anything goes!)

Side Coaching

- Don't think! Just do it!
- The topic may change, so don't plan ahead!
- Say the first thing that comes to your mind!
- Don't try to be funny!

Evaluation

- Did it get easier to respond as the game went on?
- Was there a variation in responses?
- Did response time get quicker as the players warmed up?

Challenges and Refinements

Use *Lines at a Time (on page 93)* for further improvs.

Lines at a Time

File name on CD: Lines

adjectives to describe a monster

album/CD titles

animal noises

creative mascots

creative names for babies

creative names for sports teams

excuses for being late to class

excuses for getting a speeding ticket

excuses for not turning in your homework

fantasy creatures

gemstones

hands

hockey teams (pro)

ice cream flavors

Italian food

languages

magazines

metals

Mexican food

mountain ranges

movie stars

movie titles

musical instruments

names for a pet ____

names for new TV shows

names for newly-discovered stars or planets

names for rock bands

new musical instruments

new song titles

news magazines

newspapers

operas

plays

professions/jobs

reptiles

rivers of the world

Shakespeare's plays

shapes

singers

slang expressions

soft drink flavors/brands

song titles

South American countries

sports

sports stars

states in the U.S.

strange names for superheroes

stupid compliments

synonyms for bad

synonyms for run

synonyms for walk

synonyms for good

things that are mined

things that are blue

things that are boiled

things that are found in a barnyard

things that are found in a house

things that are found in an airplane

things that are found in bodies of water

things that are fried

things that are green

things that are made of plastic

things that are made with eggs

things that are made with milk

things that are orange

things that are purple

things that are rectangular

things that are red

things that are related to holidays

things that are slimy

things that are yellow

things that begin with "q"

things that bounce

things that can get you into trouble

things that can't be bought at Wal-Mart

things that come from the sky

things that come in cans

things that contain chocolate

things that contain sugar

things that contain water

things that crawl

things that end with "n"

things that fly

things that hum or buzz

things that people drink

things that reflect light

things that roll

things that swim

things that travel on water

things that walk on two feet

titles for new rock songs

titles of children's books

titles of horror movies

trees

TV sitcoms

TV talk shows

useful household objects

vegetables

What

SPACE PREP	PLAYER PREP	PERFORMANCE
0-2	**0**	**~**
MINUTES	MINUTES	MINUTES

Use These For:

Energy Expender

Group Skills

Icebreaker

PLAYERS
3-4

Sponge

Teach and Practice:

Blocking and Conventions

Characterization

Concentration

Creativity

Ensemble Acting

Following Directions

Group Dynamics

Listening and Silence

Memorization

Non-vocal Communication

Observation

Physical Control

Plot Structure

Spontaneity

EQUIPMENT
None.

That's Life

Directions

- Divide into teams of three to four.
- One player begins the game. The director asks the player a question from the list of memory jogs.
- Two to three other players begin to act out the answer, elaborating details.
- The first player may stop the action at any time to add more characters or change the direction.
- When the scene has a satisfying conclusion, the director asks the first player if he/she has another scene that could stem from this one.
- Proceed as before.

Examples

- *The blind date:* The date shows up and seems to be charming. At the restaurant he displays appalling bad manners.
- *Extension of blind date:* A dream scene in which player one imagines what the date would have been like — for better or for worse.

Side Coaching

- Develop characters!
- Add details!
- It doesn't all have to be funny!
- Add conflicts!
- Develop conflicts into a climax!
- Find a satisfactory conclusion based on previous events!

Evaluation/Critique

- Did the scene ring true?
- Did the scene develop believable characters?
- Did the scene develop believable conflicts?
- Did the scene have a logical conclusion?

Challenges and Refinements

Use *TMATTY Situations* (page 159) for *That's* Not *Real Life*.

Be prepared. This game could go on for quite some time if it catches on!

Memory Jogs

File name on CD: MemJogs

best birthday

best job you ever had

best present

best vacation

celebrity you'd like to meet

dream car

dream house

dream job

fantasy that came true

fantasy that never came true

favorite book

favorite class

favorite movie

favorite place to visit

favorite record

favorite room in the house

favorite sibling or cousin

favorite teacher

first blind date

first date

first memory

first pet

friend as a child

friend at your present age

greatest fear

happiest moment

ideal age

ideal boyfriend/girlfriend

ideal date

least favorite teacher

most dangerous moment

most eccentric relative

most embarrassing moment

most exciting moment

secret place

something you'd like to do again

something you'd never do again

superpower you would like to have

the ideal you

what you would do if you won the lottery

worst job you ever had

worst nightmare

worst piece of advice you've ever been given

worst piece of advice you've ever given

Who

Use These For:

Energy Expender

Group Skills

Icebreaker

Sponge

PLAYERS
2

Teach and Practice:

Blocking and Conventions

Characterization

Concentration

Creativity

Ensemble Acting

Following Directions

Group Dynamics

Listening and Silence

Memorization

Non-vocal Communication

Observation

Physical Control

Plot Structure

Spontaneity

EQUIPMENT
None.

Mixed Motivations

For Discussion

- How can mixing motivations lead to conflict?
- How are some mixed motivations too bland to create interesting conflicts (examples: to bore, to calm)?
- How are some mixed motivations so volatile that the scenes can spiral out of control (example: to anger and to annoy)?
- What are the implications for scene building and playwriting?

Directions

- Divide into teams of two.
- Two players draw or are assigned one motivation each.
- The group gives the players a generic situation (see *Generic Scenes* on page 71).
- The players perform the scene emphasizing their motivations.

Examples

- A job interview in which the interviewer's motivation is to *humiliate,* and the interviewee's motivation is to *plead.*
- A first date where the girl's motivation is to *annoy* and the boy's is to *flatter.*

Side Coaching

- Establish your character using your motivation as your primary personality trait!
- Use your motivation in conjunction with the other player's to motivate conflict!
- Be clear about your motivation and how it carries the action forward!

Evaluation/Critique

- Were the motivations clear?
- Did the motivations lead to conflict?
- Did the motivations lead to the scene's conclusion?

Motivations

to amuse	to evade	to mystify
to anger	to excite	to negotiate
to annoy	to flatter	to pacify
to apologize	to flirt with	to persuade
to banish	to flummox	to plead
to belittle	to follow	to provoke
to bore	to frighten	to put down
to butter up	to gross out	to question
to calm	to humiliate	to reassure
to change	to humor	to reject
to cheer	to interrogate	to relax
to coax	to intrigue	to relieve
to confuse	to irritate	to replace
to convert	to lead on	to satisfy
to convince	to learn the truth	to seduce
to disappoint	to lecture	to sicken
to discipline	to lighten up	to stall
to disgust	to make a pass	to stymie
to distract	to make jealous	to teach
to distress	to make proud	to tease
to educate	to make suspicious	to terrify
to embarrass	to make them laugh	to torture
to enlighten	to mortify	to upset
to enrage	to motivate	to urge

SPACE PREP	PLAYER PREP	PERFORMANCE
0	**3**	**5**
MINUTES	MINUTES	MINUTES

Use These For:

Energy Expender

Group Skills

Icebreaker

Sponge

PLAYERS
2-4

Teach and Practice:

Blocking and Conventions

Characterization

Concentration

Creativity

Ensemble Acting

Following Directions

Group Dynamics

Listening and Silence

Memorization

Non-vocal Communication

Observation

Physical Control

Plot Structure

Spontaneity

EQUIPMENT

None.

Nursery Rhymes

Directions

- Divide into teams of two to four.
- Each team is given the title of a nursery rhyme. (*Optional*: The entire nursery rhyme is printed and given to the players.)
- Each team is given three minutes to develop a scene inspired by the nursery rhyme.
- Scenes may be what lead up to the incident in the rhyme, how the incident occurred, or what happened as a result of the incident.

Examples

- "Little Miss Muffett" takes place in a hospital emergency room as Miss Muffett is brought in suffering a heart attack from having seen the spider.
- "Three Blind Mice" takes place in the farmer's kitchen as the farmer and his wife plot how to rid themselves of the hated mice.
- "Humpty Dumpty" is a political event as Senator Dumpty's reputation is systematically destroyed by news reporters' questions.

Evaluation/Critique

- Was it clear which nursery rhyme was used?
- Are the characters clearly developed?
- Does the scene have a beginning, a middle, and an ending?
- Is the variation on the rhyme a clever twist?

Challenges and Refinements

- Play this game as past/present/future. What happened before the incident, during the incident, and the after the incident?
- Play the rhyme in a *Literary Style* (page 85), *Historical Moment* (page 87), or *Time Period* (page 157).

Resources

The Annotated Mother Goose by William Baring-Gould.

●com   http://www.amherst.edu/~rjyanco/literature/mothergoose/

Number this list. Ask for a number from audience.

"Nursery Rhymes
by the Numbers"

File name on CD: NR

"A tisket a tasket, a green and yellow basket"
"As I was going to St. Ives"
"As round as an apple"
"Baa, baa, black sheep"
"Blow, wind, blow!"
"Bow, wow, wow, whose dog art thou?"
"Bye, baby bunting"
"Cat came fiddling out of a barn"
"Cobbler, cobbler, mend my shoe"
"Cock-a-doodle-doo! My dame has lost her shoe"
"Come, butter, come"
"Cushy cow bonny, let down thy milk"
"Diddle, diddle, dumpling, my son John"
"Ding, dong, bell, Pussy's in the well"
"Farmer went riding upon his gray mare"
"Georgie Porgey"
"Girls and boys, come out to play"
"God bless the master of this house"
"Here we go 'round the mulberry bush"
"Hey! Diddle, Diddle, the cat and the fiddle"
"Hickory, dickory, dock"
"Higgledy, piggledy, my black hen"
"Humpty Dumpty sat on a wall"
"I had a little nut-tree, nothing would it bear"
"I had a little pony, his name was Dapple-gray"
"I have a little sister, they call her Peep, Peep"
"I saw a ship a-sailing"
"If all the seas were one sea, what a *great* sea
   they would be"
"In marble walls as white as milk"
"Intery, mintery, cutery-corn"
"Jack and Jill went up the hill"
"Jack be nimble, Jack be quick"
"Jack Sprat"
"Lady bird, lady bird, fly away home"
"Lavender's Blue"
"The Lion and the Unicorn"
"Little Betty Blue lost her holiday shoe"
"Little Bo Peep has lost her sheep"
"Little Boy Blue, come blow your horn"
"Little Jack Horner sat in a corner"
"Little King Boggen, he built a fine hall"
"Little Miss Muffet sat on a tuffet"
"Little Nancy Etticoat in a white petticoat"
"Little Robin Redbreast sat upon a rail"

"Little Tommy Tucker"
"London Bridge is falling down"
"Mistress Mary, quite contrary"
"Monday's child is fair of face"
"North wind doth blow, and we shall have snow"
"Old King Cole was a merry old soul"
"Old Mother Hubbard went to the cupboard"
"Once I saw a little bird come hop, hop, hop"
"One, two, buckle my shoe"
"Pat-a-cake, pat-a-cake, baker's man"
"Pease porridge hot, pease porridge cold"
"Peter Piper picked a peck of pickled peppers"
"Peter, Peter, Pumpkin Eater"
"Polly, put the kettle on"
"Pussycat, pussycat, where have you been?"
"Ride a cock-horse to Banbury Cross"
"Ring around the Rosie"
"Robert Rowley rolled a round roll 'round"
"Rock-a-bye, baby, in the tree top"
"The rose is red, the violet's blue"
"Rub-a-dub-dub, three men in a tub"
"Simple Simon met a pieman going to the fair"
"Sing a song of sixpence, a pocket full of rye"
"Star light, Star bright"
"The owl and the pussycat"
"The queen of hearts, she made some tarts"
"There was a crooked man, and he went a crooked mile"
"There was a little girl who had a little curl"
"There was a man in our town, and he was
   wondrous wise"
"There was an old man who lived in a wood"
"There was an old woman tossed up in a basket"
"There was an old woman who lived in a shoe"
"There were three jovial huntsmen"
"Thirty days hath September"
"This is the house that Jack built"
"This little pig when to market"
"Three Blind Mice"
"Three children sliding on the ice upon a summer's day"
"Three Little Kittens"
"To marker, to market, to buy a fat pig"
"Twenty white horses upon a red hill"
"Twinkle, Twinkle Little Star"
"Up little baby, stand up clear"
"Wee Willie Winkie runs through the town"
"Willy boy, Willy boy, where are you going?"
"Yankee Doodle"

SPACE PREP
0
MINUTES

PLAYER PREP
0
MINUTES

PERFORMANCE
~
MINUTES

I'm Going on a Trip "(Alphabetically)"

Use These For:

Energy Expender

Group Skills

Icebreaker

Sponge

PLAYERS
Full Group

Teach and Practice:

Blocking and Conventions

Characterization

Concentration

Creativity

Ensemble Acting

Following Directions

Group Dynamics

Listening and Silence

Memorization

Non-vocal Communication

Observation

Physical Control

Plot Structure

Spontaneity

EQUIPMENT
None.

Directions

- Players sit in a circle.
- The first player begins the story with "I'm going on a trip, and I'm taking a/an _____(object that begins with the letter 'a')." The player must choose an object that can be taken on a trip.
- The next player in the circle repeats the phrase "I'm going on a trip, and I'm taking a _____ (object that begins with a 'b')," and then adds the first player's object.
- The third player starts with a new object that beings with a "c" then adds the second actor's then the first actor's.

Example

- I'm going on a trip, and I'm taking an apple.
- I'm going on a trip, and I'm taking a baseball bat and an apple.
- I'm going on a trip, and I'm taking my cat, a baseball bat, and an apple.

Side Coaching

- You have to listen as well as think of your own word!
- Listen to the person just before you!
- No helping. Each of you needs to remember your own part.

Challenges and Refinements

- Go around the circle more than once.
- Speed up the process. Allow no more than a set number of seconds for players to respond.

Evaluation/Critique

- Strategize on how they will play the game better next time. Remind everyone to listen to what is going on around them.
- Have players think about how to memorize. Some people are better than others at memorizing. Have the players who were the best at the game tell how they did it. This may be the first time actors actually think about the memorization process.

Bonus

The director sees how well individual players memorize in order to cast them in a scripted play.

Competition

Objects

artificial flowers
artificial sweetener
ashtray
ballet shoe
balloons
bar of soap
barrette
baseball cap
basket
basketball
bathtub
belt
bird's nest
book
bookends
boom box
boot
bottle of perfume
Brazil nut
briefcase
bubble gum
bud vase
button
candle
candy bar
candy dish
cassette tape
CD
cellophane tape
chain saw
chalkboard eraser
chewing gum
cigar box
clipboard
clock
coasters
coat
Coca-Cola
coffee can
coins
compact disc
computer
computer diskette
costume jewelry
crayons
credit card
crowbar

cup
dental floss
dentist's drill
dictionary
Diet Pepsi
Dr. Pepper
drinking straw
driver's license
dustpan
earmuffs
egg
electric drill
encyclopedia
envelope
eraser
Excalibur
eyeglasses
feather duster
felt marker
fire extinguisher
flashlight
flower
fork
fountain pen
frying pan
glass
glass jar
gloves
Hacky Sack
hairbrush
hand lotion
hand mirror
hand puppet
handkerchief
hat
key chain
keys
knitting needle
Koosh Ball
lampshade
library card
light bulb
lottery ticket
magazine
marble
marionette
mask

measuring cup
metal file
mixing bowl
model airplane
monkey wrench
nail file
napkins
National Enquirer
Nerf Ball
newspaper
paddle
paper bag
paper clip
paper cups
pen
pencil
pencil case
pepper shaker
picture frame
playing cards
postcards
puppy dog
purple dinosaur
purse
rags
ribbons
roll of tape
rosebud
rubber ball
rubber band
rubber chicken
ruler
safe
salamander
salt shaker
saucer
scarf
school bus
scissors
script
shoehorn
shoelaces
show
silver picture frame
Smurf
soap dish
spoon

stapler
steel wool pad
stethoscope
stick of chewing gum
sticky note
straw
stuffed animal
sunglasses
sword
tap shoes
tape measure
tea bags
tea strainer
teddy bear
telephone
telephone book
ten dollar bill
thermometer
thesaurus
ticket stub
tie
tie clip
tissues
toothbrush
toothpick
tuna fish can
umbrella
veil
Wall Street Journal
wallet
washcloth
whistle
wire hanger
wristwatch
yardstick
zoology textbook

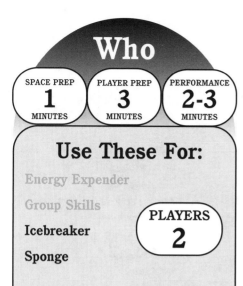

SPACE PREP
1
MINUTES

PLAYER PREP
3
MINUTES

PERFORMANCE
2-3
MINUTES

Use These For:

Energy Expender

Group Skills

Icebreaker

Sponge

PLAYERS
2

Teach and Practice:

Blocking and Conventions

Characterization

Concentration

Creativity

Ensemble Acting

Following Directions

Group Dynamics

Listening and Silence

Memorization

Non-vocal Communication

Observation

Physical Control

Plot Structure

Spontaneity

EQUIPMENT
Assorted tables, chairs, and props as available and needed.

Obsessed With

Directions

- Divide into teams of two.
- The players think of, draw, or are assigned an obsession.
- The group gives the players a place (*Places* on page 119) or a title (*Film Titles* on page 61 or *Clichés* on page 29) for the scene.
- Players have three minutes to plan and set up for the scene.
- As the scene progresses, the players gradually become more and more obsessed.

Example

- The players meet in a nightclub. They are two women out on the town. The first is obsessed with *the opposite sex*. This really bugs the other woman who is obsessed with *noise*.
- The players act out the title, *The Very Bad Day*. They are two co-workers who have had a problem with their boss and are discussing it over drinks after work. One is obsessed with *money*, which is making him upset at the choice of the meeting place. The other is obsessed with *gossip* and wants to destroy the boss's reputation.

Side Coaching

- Play your obsession!
- Remember: there's a plot, too!
- React to the other's obsession and try to build it into your relationship!
- Let the obsessions carry the plot forward.

Evaluation/Critique

- How were the obsessions incorporated into the characters' personalities?
- Did the obsessions contribute to the conflicts/conclusion?

Challenges and Refinements

- Obsessions may be played for comedy by total exaggeration.
- Obsessions may be played seriously by making them subtle but annoying to the other player.

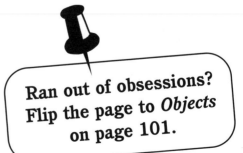

Ran out of obsessions? Flip the page to *Objects* on page 101.

Obsessions

aches and pains
alien abductions
American Idol
animals
annoying people
backpacking
baking
baking cookies
being on time
being on top
being overly friendly
being secretive
biting fingernails
buying magazines
C-SPAN
camping
celebrity couples
championing the underdog
children
Chinese food
chocolate
collectibles
collecting stuffed animals
the color blue
combing their hair
complaining
Court TV
criticizing others
digital cameras
downloading music
drinking coffee
drinking soda
eating snails
exercise
fashions
finishing others' sentences
food
furniture

genealogy
germs
getting negative attention
getting straight As
giggling
gossip
guns
horoscopes
hosts' quirks
humming
hunting
instant messaging
insulting people
Jerry Springer
Judy Garland
journaling
knowing other people's business
lost causes
love
makeup
model railroads
money
mountain biking
movie stars
movies
MP3 players
music
nitpicking
noise
numerology
opposite sex
people's shoes
platform shoes
playing cards
playing Hacky Sack
politics
popping pimples
putting on lotion

Queer Eye for the Straight Guy
sports statistics
mystery novels
reality TV
redecorating the house
roller coasters
running
skateboarding
smells
snowboarding
soap operas
songs from musicals
spandex
Starbucks
thumb sucking
surfing the net
taking care of people
talking about working out
teeth
the news
their own nails
their toes
video games
wearing hats
wearing pocket protectors
wearing the color blue
weather
weight
winning
woodworking
working out

SPACE PREP
2
MINUTES

PLAYER PREP
0
MINUTES

PERFORMANCE
<5
MINUTES

Use These For:

Energy Expender

Group Skills

Icebreaker

Sponge

PLAYERS
4

Teach and Practice:

Blocking and Conventions

Characterization

Concentration

Creativity

Ensemble Acting

Following Directions

Group Dynamics

Listening and Silence

Memorization

Non-vocal Communication

Observation

Physical Control

Plot Structure

Spontaneity

EQUIPMENT
4 chairs or stools.

What's My Line?

Directions

- Divide into teams of four. The director chooses one player from a team to be the host.
- Each of the remaining three players is endowed with an occupation that only the group and the host know.
- One at a time the players enter the talk show scene and are interviewed about their jobs. Since the players do not know what their jobs are, the answers can be quite humorous.
- Players must try to adapt to reactions to their answers, eventually discovering their endowed occupation.

Side Coaching

- Players: Answer boldly as if you know your occupation!
- Players: Don't be tentative!
- Players: Avoid seeming lost. Play it realistically!
- Host: Ask specific direct questions without revealing the occupations too quickly!
- Host: Don't spend all your time on one player. Divide the questions among all three!

Evaluation/Critique

- Which kinds of questions elicited the most specific responses?
- How did the players eventually catch on?
- What kinds of questions worked best to help guess the guest's occupation?
- How did the guest avoid telling his or her occupation?
- What kind of physical changes did he undergo?

Challenges and Refinements

- The players all know their occupations, and the host must ask questions to guess their occupations.
- The group does not know the occupations and may ask questions.
- Instead of using occupations, use hobbies.
- Five panelists endow three guests with occupations. (The guests do not know their own occupations.) The panelists ask questions of the guests, gently leading them to guess their own occupations. (See *Talk Show Game II* on page 47.)

This game can really get a group involved! The only problem with opening it up for questions is that some tend to give it away to friends.

Occupations

accountant

actor

acupuncturist

advertising salesperson

aerobics teacher

air conditioning installer

aircraft pilot

amusement park ride operator

antique bookseller

antique coin merchant

antique dealer

appliance repairperson

archaeologist

architect

arson investigator

art dealer

art thief

artist

ASL signer

astronaut

auctioneer

auto body repairperson

bacteriologist

bail bondsman

bank teller

banker

bareback rider

baseball umpire

bicycle racer

blacksmith

blood bank worker

bomb squad member

boxer

bronco buster

burglar

burglar alarm installer

cable guy

calligrapher

candy maker

card shark

carpenter

carpet cleaner

caterer

Center for Disease
   Control doctor

chambermaid

character actor

chef

chimney sweep

chorus girl

cigar maker

circus ringmaster

civil engineer

closet designer

clown

comedy writer

commodities trader

computer technician

concrete truck driver

construction flag person

contractor

cook

cosmetologist

counselor

country-western singer

cowboy

critter getter

croupier

cruise ship captain

custodian

dancer

daytime drama actor

dentist

department store
   clothing buyer

detective

diamond cutter

doctor

dog trainer

dowser/water witch

drill sergeant

economist

electrician

engineer

entertainment hypnotist

exotic dancer

farmer

Occupations

fashion designer

FedEx driver

fiction writer

film editor

fine art appraiser

firefighter

fisherman

flight attendant

florist

fortune-teller

gardener

glassblower

golfer

gunsmith

hairdresser

headstone carver

health club manager

herpetologist

highway patrol officer

historian

hit man

hockey player

homeless shelter worker

hospice nurse

hot air balloon pilot

hot shot firefighter

hotel manager

house painter

housekeeper

hypnotherapist

indoor gardener

insurance salesman

interior designer

investment counselor

jailer

jewel thief

jeweler

journalist

juggler

juror

landscaper

language translator

law clerk

lawyer

librarian

lighthouse keeper

lion tamer

loan officer

locksmith

long haul trucker

lumberjack

mailroom employee

maitre d' hotel

makeup artist

martial arts expert

massage therapist

matchmaker

mattress salesperson

member of a boy band

meter reader

miner

minister

motorcycle rider

mountaineer

movie stuntman

MRI operator

musician

nanny

newscaster

Olympic swimmer

orthodontist

orthopedic surgeon

painter

party planner

personal trainer

pest control specialist

pet groomer

pet store owner

photographer

pizza deliverer

plastic surgeon

plumber

policeman

politician

pool maintenance person

postal worker

potter

preschool teacher

priest

principal

professional golfer

professional poker player

professional wrestler

profiler

psychiatrist

puppeteer

rabbi

radio announcer

rancher

real estate agent

record producer

restaurant server

retired kindergarten teacher

rocket scientist

Rockette

roofer

sailor

school bus driver

scientist

sculptor

seamstress

service animal trainer

ship steward

shopkeeper

shoplifter

short-order cook

sideshow barker

singer

ski bum

snow cone maker

software developer

soldier

sports announcer

spy

stand-up comic

Starbucks barista

storyteller

sumo wrestler

supermodel

talk show host

tattoo artist

taxi driver

taxidermist

teacher

telegraph operator

televangelist

temporary employee

terrorist

theatrical producer

tightrope walker

tow truck driver

travel agent

tree farmer

tree surgeon

typist

undercover FBI agent

undertaker

university professor

used car salesperson

vacuum cleaner salesperson

ventriloquist

veterinarian

videographer

warehouse person

weatherman

Web page designer

wedding planner

wedding singer

weight loss counselor

wigmaker

wine merchant

zookeeper

What

SPACE PREP	PLAYER PREP	PERFORMANCE
0 MINUTES	**0** MINUTES	**2-3** MINUTES

Use These For:

Energy Expender

Group Skills

Icebreaker

Sponge

PLAYERS 2

Teach and Practice:

Blocking and Conventions

Characterization

Concentration

Creativity

Ensemble Acting

Following Directions

Group Dynamics

Listening and Silence

Memorization

Non-vocal Communication

Observation

Physical Control

Plot Structure

Spontaneity

EQUIPMENT
None.

Opening and Closing Scenes

Directions

- Divide into teams of two.
- Each pair is given, draws, or is assigned an opening or a closing scene.
- The players improvise the scene that takes place after the opening or before the closing scene.

Example

- Opening Scene: *Wanders around the room crying*. Player A wanders around the scene crying. Player B enters and tells A that at least the thieves didn't take the jewelry hidden in the third shoebox from the right in the closet. Player A counters with that fact that the thieves did get all of the family photographs, and they broke the only dish that their great-grandmother had given them. The scene develops with the two players examining what is really important in life.

- Closing Scene: *Falls asleep in a chair*. The scene begins with Players A and B playing an indoor game of hide and seek. A is a child, and B is a grandparent trying to occupy A until A's parents arrive. There is a decided energy level gap. B tries to keep up with the energetic youngster but gets more tired by the minute. Finally, B convinces A to tell a story and falls asleep in a chair as A spins a long and involved make-believe story.

Side Coaching

- Don't forget where you have come from/must get to!
- Remember: there must be characterization, too!
- Listen and respond appropriately!

Evaluation/Critique

- Did the rest of the scene logically follow the opening scene or lead up to the closing scene?
- Did you see a logical plot evolve?
- Were the characters clear?

Challenges and Refinements

- The players are given *both* an opening and a closing scene.
- Solo performers pantomime selected opening and closing scenes.

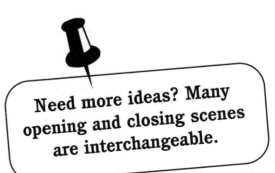

Need more ideas? Many opening and closing scenes are interchangeable.

Opening and Closing Scenes

Opening Scenes

Answers phone.

Calls for dog and pets it.

Comes in looking through the mail.

Dances around the room.

Dusts furniture while singing happily.

Enters carrying a tray, trips, and drops it.

Enters combing hair.

Enters dragging a body.

Enters, hears a noise, and jumps.

Enters, looks under the couch, shrugs, sits down.

Enters, starts to sneeze.

Enters, turns on all the lights.

Goes to closet, puts on coat.

Goes to closet, rummages through, and slams door shut.

Goes to mirror, makes faces.

Goes to phone and shouts into it.

Goes to window and looks out.

Goes to window and opens it.

Goes to window and screams.

Paces back and forth across the room.

Picks up newspaper, settles in chair with feet up.

Picks up phone and checks messages.

Screams, jumps on chair.

Searches for a pen and paper, finds it, and starts to write.

Sits in chair, opens a book.

Sits in chair, suddenly jumps up.

Sits in chair, turns on TV.

Sneaks in, hides behind chair.

Sneaks in, picks up a book, hides it under coat.

Sprays room with air freshener.

Starts to floss teeth.

Straightens room while scowling.

Tears an article out of the paper.

Types on computer, gets frustrated.

Wanders around crying.

Closing Scenes

Blows a whistle.

Calls frantically for help.

Covers eyes.

Crawls on hands and knees across the room.

Drops a purse or briefcase and runs.

Falls asleep in chair.

Goes to the window and looks out.

Looks around wildly and freezes.

Opens a drawer and takes out a letter.

Opens door, looks around.

Opens the door and screams.

Picks up a magazine and throws it down again.

Picks up an envelope and opens it.

Picks up an envelope and puts a stamp on it.

Puts a tape in the VCR.

Puts hand in mouth.

Rushes out of the room.

Searches around the room and freezes.

Shakes head sadly.

Shrugs shoulders, leaves.

Sinks into a chair and covers face with hands.

Sips a cup of coffee.

Sits in chair and turns on TV.

Slowly opens the refrigerator door.

Slowly picks up the telephone.

Slowly sinks to the floor.

Sneezes and claps hand to mouth.

Sprays pepper spray.

Tears up a letter.

Throws a book across the room.

Tries not to throw up, but does.

Turns off the computer.

Turns off the light and leaves the room.

Turns on the computer.

Whirls around and freezes with hands up.

SPACE PREP
0
MINUTES

PLAYER PREP
0
MINUTES

PERFORMANCE
5
MINUTES

As If ...

Use These For:

Energy Expender

Group Skills

Icebreaker

PLAYERS
Full Group

Sponge

Teach and Practice:

Blocking and Conventions

Characterization

Concentration

Creativity

Ensemble Acting

Following Directions

Group Dynamics

Listening and Silence

Memorization

Non-vocal Communication

Observation

Physical Control

Plot Structure

Spontaneity

EQUIPMENT

None.

Directions

- The entire group spreads out across the room.
- The director instructs them to perform a pantomime "as if ..."
- After thirty seconds to a minute, the director changes the pantomime.
- This activity continues for about five minutes or until the group loses focus.

Side Coaching

- Just do it!
- Don't watch anyone else!
- Make your movements specific!
- Add details!

Examples

- In the same emotion: Watching a sad movie; writing a Dear John letter; writing and mailing a letter; taking the SAT.
- In chronological order: hiking in the woods, climbing a hill, picking up sticks, and building a campfire.

Evaluation/Critique

- Which pantomimes were easiest for you? Why?
- Was it hard to switch focus?

Challenges and Refinements

- Develop a scene based on one of the pantomimes.
- Develop a scene incorporating all of the pantomimes.
- Stop the action and have the group focus on a particularly good example.

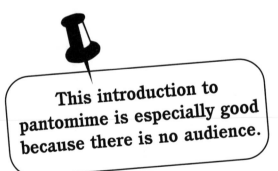

This introduction to pantomime is especially good because there is no audience.

Pantomime Ideas

File name on CD: PantoIdeas

As if you were ...

arranging a bookshelf

arranging flowers

baking a cake

breaking and re-gluing a vase

breaking into a house

breaking into your house

brewing coffee

brushing your teeth

building a campfire

burping a baby

changing a cloth diaper

changing a flat tire on a car

chasing an escaped puppy

cheating on a test

checking yourself for ticks

cleaning your room

climbing a hill

dancing when you think no one sees you

deep-sea fishing

delivering the mail through yards of unfriendly dogs

driving a car

eating spaghetti

feeding a pet

finding a seat in the middle of a crowded row

flying a kite

flying a kite in a storm

getting "mystery meat" on your tray in the cafeteria

getting a "Dear John" letter

getting a spider out of the bathtub

getting ready for the prom

hanging a picture

having a tooth pulled

hiking in the woods

knitting

learning a dance step

learning to ride a bike

learning to walk

listening to music you don't like

listening to music you like

making a peanut butter sandwich

moving a refrigerator

negotiating your way across a toy-littered room

painting a picture

painting a portrait

painting your toenails

passing a note in class

picking up a poisonous snake

picking up a snake

piecing together a jigsaw puzzle

planting a rosebush

playing a sport

playing an instrument

pulling a loose thread

putting in contact lenses

putting on a wet swimsuit

putting on makeup

putting together a complicated toy

reading a love letter

reading a love letter to someone else

rearranging furniture

rehearsing a love scene

riding a roller coaster with an upset stomach

searching for a lost house key

setting the table

shopping in an exclusive clothing store

singing in the shower

smelling something suspicious

snow skiing

styling your hair

swimming

taking a driver's test

taking a hearing test

taking a multiple-choice test

taking icky medicine

taking out the trash

taking the SAT

teaching a dance step

teaching someone how to play an instrument

teaching someone to swim

threading a needle

trying not to bite your fingernails

trying not to scratch an itch

trying on clothes

trying to avoid going on a roller coaster

trying to get a baby to sleep

trying to pay attention in church

trying to put a noncompliant child to bed

trying to put on pantyhose that are too small

trying to resist a fattening dessert

trying to stay awake in a boring class

trying to swat a fly

trying to use a sewing machine

turning on a computer and using it

using chopsticks for the first time

waiting for a doctor

waiting for the mailman

waiting for the phone to ring

waiting in a long line for an amusement park ride

walking a dog

walking four dogs

washing a dog

washing dishes

washing your car

watching a sad movie

watching a scary movie

watching an action movie

window-shopping

working out at the gym

writing a "Dear John" letter

writing and mailing a letter

Need more ideas? Try *Opening and Closing Scenes* on page 109.

SPACE PREP
3
MINUTES

PLAYER PREP
3
MINUTES

PERFORMANCE
3-5
MINUTES

Use These For:

Energy Expender

Group Skills

Icebreaker

Sponge

PLAYERS
4

Teach and Practice:

Blocking and Conventions

Characterization

Concentration

Creativity

Ensemble Acting

Following Directions

Group Dynamics

Listening and Silence

Memorization

Non-vocal Communication

Observation

Physical Control

Plot Structure

Spontaneity

EQUIPMENT
Assorted tables, chairs
and props as available
and needed.

Past/Present/Future

Directions

- Divide into teams of four.
- Choose a *Generic Scene* from page 71 (example: *first date*) and a place suitable for time travel (*Places* on page 119).
- The teams think of, draw, or are assigned a time in the past.

Game 1
The teams improvise the scene as it would be in the past, in the present, and in a future of their choosing.

Game 2
Have three teams, one showing the scene in the past, one showing the scene in the present, and one showing the scene in the future.

Game 3
Choose a *Historical Moment* (page 87) and have different teams perform the generic scene in the time of that event. Perform the scenes chronologically.

Evaluation/Critique

- Did the plots effectively show how each time period affected the situation?
- Did the players fit your idea of how people would have behaved in the time period?
- Was the language used suitable to your understanding of the time period?

Evaluation/Critique

- Coordinate with history or literature classes to fit in with historical units in the curriculum.
- As a class, make lists of past times jogs (Roaring Twenties: short swingy skirts, women's short hair, bathtub gin, speakeasies, the Charleston, gangsters.)

17th century

18th century

19th century

20th century

21st century

Bronze Age

Civil War

Commonwealth (Cromwell)

Dark Ages

Edwardian Era

Elizabethan Era

French Revolution

Great Depression

Hundred Years War

Industrial Revolution

Iron Age

Jacobean Period

Korean War

Middle Ages

Napoleonic Era

Neanderthal Period

Prehistory

Reformation

Regency Period

Renaissance

Revolutionary War

Roaring Twenties

Romantic Period

Russian Revolution

Spanish-American War

Stone Age

Victorian Era

Vietnam war

War of 1812

War of the Roses

Who

SPACE PREP
2
MINUTES

PLAYER PREP
3
MINUTES

PERFORMANCE
3
MINUTES

Use These For:

Energy Expender

Group Skills

Icebreaker

Sponge

PLAYERS
2

Teach and Practice:

Blocking and Conventions

Characterization

Concentration

Creativity

Ensemble Acting

Following Directions

Group Dynamics

Listening and Silence

Memorization

Non-vocal Communication

Observation

Physical Control

Plot Structure

Spontaneity

EQUIPMENT
Assorted tables, chairs and props as available and needed.

Annoyance Game

Directions

- Divide into teams of two.
- Two players start a *Generic Scene* (page 71).
- After the scene has started, each player draws a pet peeve from the director.
- During the course of the scene, the annoying habit should escalate and help further the plot.

Example

- In the scene, *The Breakup*, the boy is breaking up with the girl. His annoying habit is *chewing gum* and hers is *whining*. As the scene progresses, he blows bigger and bigger bubbles which she complains about more and more.
- In *The Job Interview*, the employer interviews a prospective employee for a job as a cashier. The employer's habit is *bullying*; the interviewee's is *lying*. He keeps challenging her résumé as she elaborates more and more.

Side Coaching

- Play your annoying habit!
- Exaggerate!
- Use it to annoy the other person!
- Use it as a way to further the plot and to resolve the scene!

Evaluation/Critique

- Were the habits somewhat believable?
- Did the habit further the scene's conflicts?
- Did the habits help resolve the scene? (Example: the employer bullies the prospective employee so much that she confesses that she has never had a job and never wants one.)

Challenges and Refinements

- Play the habits for subtlety.
- Switch habits (as in *Status Slide* on page 150).

bad manners

being prejudiced

bragging

bribing

brown nosing

bullying

cheating

chewing gum

clumsiness

cutting in line

drinking too much

elbowing

exaggerating

hitting

ignoring others

interrupting

loud talking

lying

making assumptions

nose picking

poor oral hygiene

pushing

shoving

smoking

standing too close

stealing

talking while others are talking

wearing inappropriate clothing

wearing too-tight clothing

whining

Need more pet peeves? Try *Annoying Personal Habits* on page 17.

SPACE PREP	PLAYER PREP	PERFORMANCE
0	0	<5
MINUTES	MINUTES	MINUTES

Use These For:

Energy Expender

Group Skills

Icebreaker

Sponge

PLAYERS
Full Group

Teach and Practice:

Blocking and Conventions

Characterization

Concentration

Creativity

Ensemble Acting

Following Directions

Group Dynamics

Listening and Silence

Memorization

Non-vocal Communication

Observation

Physical Control

Plot Structure

Spontaneity

EQUIPMENT
None.

The Where Game

Directions

- The group stands in a large circle.
- One player thinks of, draws, or is assigned the name of a fantasy or real location (See *Places* on page 119).
- The player goes to the center of the circle and starts an activity associated with that location.
- One at a time, other players volunteer to come in and add to the scene establishing other landmarks in the location. Each player furthers the plot.

Example

- The location is a *cemetery*. The first player enters and begins digging a grave. Other players come in putting flowers on headstones and mowing around the graves.
- The location is a *playground*. The first player enters and begins playing in a sandbox. Other players join in by swinging on the swings or playing on a teeter-totter.

Side Coaching

- Establish landmarks in the location!
- Interact with the landmarks as well as the characters inhabiting the location!
- Try to develop a plot!
- Add conflict where you can!

Evaluation/Critique

- Were you clear where you were?
- Were the landmarks in the place well established?
- Were the landmarks used to further the plot?

Challenges and Refinements

- Players draw a location and place a specific scene there.
  - *Example:* Park Bench — First date.
  - *Example:* Movie Theatre — Breakup of a romance.

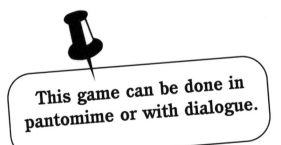

This game can be done in pantomime or with dialogue.

Tap In (Milwaukee Freeze Tag)

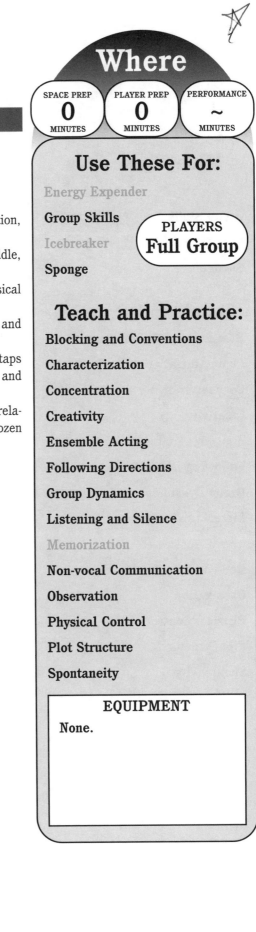

Directions

- The players sit in a circle.
- Two volunteers start the game in the center of the circle.
- The audience suggests or the director assigns a starting place, time, situation, characters, line, etc.
- Starting with the prompt, the players create a scene with a beginning, middle, and end.
- When the players have established the plot and are in an interesting physical position, the director calls, "freeze." The actors freeze immediately.
- The director assigns a new player. The assigned player enters the circle and selects a player to replace.
- After studying the exact position of the actor to be replaced, the new player taps that player's shoulder. The replaced player leaves the middle of the circle, and the new player adopts the replaced player's position.
- The new player now starts a *new* improv based on the established physical relationship from the previous scene. In one line the new player gives the frozen actor enough information to participate.
- The process repeats until the director calls "freeze" again.

Side Coaching

- Really look at the position you will be taking!
- Give information — don't ask questions when you start your new scene!
- You have to go with the information you get or make getting it part of your scene!
- It doesn't have to be funny!
- Don't stop. Keep going until I call, "freeze!"

Evaluation/Critique

- What did you like and why?
- Could the audience tell what the new scenes were right away?
- Did the new players establish who and where they were quickly?
- Did the new players establish what they were doing?

Use These For:

Energy Expender

Group Skills

Icebreaker

Sponge

PLAYERS Full Group

Teach and Practice:

Blocking and Conventions

Characterization

Concentration

Creativity

Ensemble Acting

Following Directions

Group Dynamics

Listening and Silence

Memorization

Non-vocal Communication

Observation

Physical Control

Plot Structure

Spontaneity

EQUIPMENT

None.

Helpful lists for *Tap In: Places* – page 119; *Past Times* – page 113; *Pantomime Ideas* – page 111; *Generic Scenes* – page 71; *Famous People* – page 59; *First Line, Last Line* – page 63.

Where

SPACE PREP
0
MINUTES

PLAYER PREP
0
MINUTES

PERFORMANCE
1-3
MINUTES

Use These For:

Energy Expender

Group Skills

Icebreaker

Sponge

PLAYERS
2

Teach and Practice:

Blocking and Conventions

Characterization

Concentration

Creativity

Ensemble Acting

Following Directions

Group Dynamics

Listening and Silence

Memorization

Non-vocal Communication

Observation

Physical Control

Plot Structure

Spontaneity

EQUIPMENT
None.

In A ... With A ...

Directions

- Divide into teams of two.
- The teams are assigned or draw the name of a place and an object (See *Objects* on page 101).
- The players have a set amount of time (one to three minutes is usually sufficient) to act out a scene that uses the object and place. The scene must have a coherent plot that contains a beginning, a middle, and an ending.
- The director or a timer alerts the players when there are ten seconds remaining in the allotted improv time.

Examples

- In an ice cream parlor with a pencil.
- In a grocery store with a pizza box.

Side Coaching

- Don't take time to think. Just play it!
- Trust your partner!
- You can do it, just let it flow!

Evaluation/Critique

- Could the audience tell where the team was?
- Did they establish where they were quickly?
- Did they establish who they were?
- What was the object?
- Did they use their time well?

Challenges and Refinements

- The game becomes *In A ... With A ... Without A ...* with the addition of another object.

For more ideas, see *Rooms in a House* on page 135.

General Places

aircraft carrier

ancient Indian burial ground

archeology excavation

auto mechanic's garage

automobile junkyard

backstage

bank vault

barnyard

basement of an abandoned building

basketball court

bench at a fountain in Rome

biosphere

boardwalk at a beach

boxing ring

cab of a semi truck

candy counter at a general store

car racetrack

carpenter's workshop

cattle judging ring at a state fair

cockpit of a jet airliner

college dorm room

commuter train at rush hour

computer technician's workshop

concert hall, front row, center seat

cornfield

dance floor at a popular club

deep sea fishing boat

deserted beach on a remote island

diner kitchen at breakfast time

doll maker's studio

dressing room of an elegant clothing store

dude ranch corral

edge of a bridge over a 500-foot deep gorge

electrician's workshop

empty football stadium

empty locker room

fallout shelter

fire escape of a theatre

fishing dock/pier

furniture showroom

general store/post office in a small southern town

graphic artist's studio

graveyard

greenhouse

helicopter over a large city

highway construction site

horse racing track

hospital ER

intensive care hospital room

jail cell in a large police station

landfill

large city police station

Las Vegas casino gambling floor

Mars

maternity hospital room

MD examination room

middle of a dense forest

midway at the fair

modern art museum

modern artist's studio

moon

motocross track

movie theatre restroom

museum dinosaur collection

musician's recording studio

mystery shelves of a bookstore

new car showroom

newspaper newsroom

ocean liner at sea

old-fashioned soda fountain

one-horse sleigh

outdoor basketball court

parking lot of a baseball stadium

playground

plumber's workshop

portrait artist's studio

prairie

press box at a pro football stadium

Queen's bedroom

railway tunnel

rain forest

restaurant kitchen at dinnertime

restroom of an elegant restaurant

Places

rose garden

sewer

shopping mall basement

side-wheeler boat

skateboard park half pipe

small town police station

snow-covered road on a hill

spaceship heading to Jupiter

space shuttle in orbit

submarine torpedo tube

summit of a 10,000-foot mountain

taxicab at rush hour

television newsroom during broadcast

tropical jungle

volcano

water park ride

wax museum

x-ray room

Specific Places

Alcatraz

Amazon River

Amsterdam

Angor Wat

Antarctica

Arc de Triomphe

Australian Outback

Badlands, Montana

Bald Mountain

Berlin Wall

Bermuda Triangle

Bikini Atoll

Biosphere

Black Forest

Black Hole of Calcutta

Bourbon Street, New Orleans

Cairo

Cape Canaveral

Central Park, NYC

Chesapeake Bay

Chichen Itza

Copenhagen

Dallas

Dead Man's Gulch

Death Valley

Devil's Island

Dodge City

Donner Pass

Eiffel Tower

Elba Island

Ellis Island

Everglades

French Riviera

Gettysburg

Golden Gate Bridge

Great Plains

Great Pyramid

Great Smokey Mountains

Guam

Guggenheim Museum

Harrod's Department Store

Havana, Cuba

Hiroshima

Hollywood

Hong Kong Harbor

Indian reservation

Kennedy Space Center

King Tut's tomb

Land's End, England

Lapland

Last Chance Saloon

l'Hermitage, St. Petersburg

Library of Congress

Little America

Little Big Horn

London

Long Island Gold Coast

Machu Pichu

Macy's Department Store

Matterhorn

Metropolitan Opera House, NYC

Mississippi River

Mongolia

Monterey Bay Aquarium

Mt. St. Helens

Nepal

Neuschwanstein

Niagara Falls

Nile River

Places

Norwegian Fjords

Oklahoma

Old Lady Leery's barn, Chicago

Oslo, Norway

Panama Canal

Paris

Parthenon, Athens

Pearl Harbor

Pebble Beach Golf Course

Puerto Rico

Queen Elizabeth II Conference Centre

Queen of England's bedroom

Rock of Gibraltar

Roman Coliseum

Roswell, New Mexico

Sahara Desert

San Diego Zoo

Shark Tank at Sea World

Sherwood Forest

Siberia

Sidney, Australia

South Beach

South Seas

Spanish Steps, Rome

Statue of Liberty

Supreme Court courtroom

Swiss Alps

Taj Mahal

Tasmania

Tiajuana

Tibetan Lamasery

Tierra del Fuego

Tokyo

Tower of London

Trading floor of the New York Stock Exchange

Tuscon

U.S. Capitol

Valley of the Kings, Egypt

Waikiki

Washington Monument

Waterloo

White House

Wrigley Field

Yosemite Park

Fantasy and Unusual Places

anthill

beach in the Jurassic era

center of the earth

checkerboard

clock

Clue (game)

galaxy far, far away

human brain

jousting tournament

lost city of Atlantis

Middle Earth

Monopoly (game)

Neverland

pirate ship

robot factory

someone else's body

the Catacombs

through the looking glass

torturer's dungeon

UFO

under the sea

your stomach

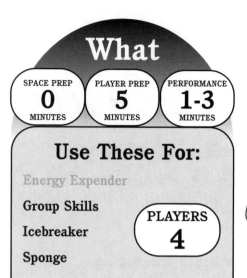

Use These For:

Energy Expender

Group Skills

Icebreaker

Sponge

PLAYERS
4

Teach and Practice:

Blocking and Conventions

Characterization

Concentration

Creativity

Ensemble Acting

Following Directions

Group Dynamics

Listening and Silence

Memorization

Non-vocal Communication

Observation

Physical Control

Plot Structure

Spontaneity

EQUIPMENT
None.

Eureka!

Directions

- Divide into teams of four.
- Each team draws or is assigned a problem that needs solving.
- The team gets five minutes to plan a scene that solves the problem.
- The team then gets one to three minutes to perform the scene.

Examples

- *Why do dogs chase cats?* The scene starts with talking dogs and cats living and playing in harmony. Suddenly the cats play a sneaky trick on the dogs. The dogs are so hurt that from then on they chase the cats whenever they see them.
- *Why is the FBI covering up what happened in Roswell?* The scene starts with the aliens landing and meeting the FBI who are ready to attack them. The aliens capture the FBI agents, take them in their ship, and put implants in their brains, which lead the agents to claim that aliens never landed. The aliens then infiltrate the FBI.

Evaluation/Critique

- Was the problem solved?
- Did the solution seem plausible?
- Did the scene have a beginning, a middle, and an ending?

Options:
invention?

Problems That Need Solving

File name on CD: Problems

Did man evolve from monkeys?

Does astrology really work?

How can I strike it rich?

How did St. Patrick chase the snakes out of Ireland?

Who stole the cookie from the cookie jar?

Who wrote Shakespeare's plays?

Whodunit?

Why are babies born bald?

Why are dollars green?

Why are men from Mars?

Why are men usually bigger than women?

Why are there bad hair days?

Why are there seasons?

Why are there telephone solicitors?

Why can't I get rid of the spam on my computer?

Why can't I win the lottery?

Why do bad guys wear black?

Why do dogs bark before an earthquake?

Why do dogs chase cats?

Why do good guys wear white?

Why do I always get sick on roller coasters?

Why do I gain weight when I look at a piece of chocolate cake?

Why do kids beg for candy on Halloween?

Why do people smoke?

Why do Scotsmen wear kilts?

Why do we have Mondays?

Why do we have to go to school?

Why do witches fly on broomsticks?

Why does fattening food taste better?

Why does pepper make you sneeze?

Why does sugar make you hyper?

Why does the telephone always ring when I'm in the shower?

Why doesn't Communism work?

Why don't I look good in green?

Why don't kids like to read?

Why is it cold in the winter?

Why is it unlucky to walk under a ladder?

Why is the FBI covering up what happened in Roswell?

Why is the sky blue?

SPACE PREP
0
MINUTES

PLAYER PREP
3
MINUTES

PERFORMANCE
<1
MINUTES

Use These For:

Energy Expender

Group Skills

Icebreaker

PLAYERS
5

Sponge

Teach and Practice:

Blocking and Conventions

Characterization

Concentration

Creativity

Ensemble Acting

Following Directions

Group Dynamics

Listening and Silence

Memorization

Non-vocal Communication

Observation

Physical Control

Plot Structure

Spontaneity

EQUIPMENT
Assorted props.

Props Freeze

Directions

- Divide into teams of five.
- Director gives each team one prop.
- The teams have three minutes to plan three different frozen pictures using the prop as a different object in each.

Examples

- A *stethoscope* becomes an attacking snake, a crack from an earthquake, and an expensive necklace.
- A *rubber chicken* becomes the Great God Chick being worshipped by the natives, an overcooked Thanksgiving turkey, and a teddy bear.

Evaluation/Critique

- Was it clear what the prop was supposed to be?
- Was the prop the focus of the freeze?
- Did the freeze show action?

Challenges and Refinements

- A warm-up for this activity may start by using the object as it actually is.
- Bring the scene to life. Use the prop in different genre scenes (the knitting needle in a sitcom, a horror movie, and a kiddy show).

Props

The following props are helpful to both classroom teachers and the leaders of groups who regularly use improv exercises. The items on this list can be accumulated gradually and augmented with group favorites.

aluminum foil	clock	gloves	pen
artificial flowers	coasters	golf club	pencil
artificial sweetener	coat	Hacky Sack	pencil case
ashtray	coffee can	hairbrush	picture frame
ballet slipper	coffee mug	hand lotion	purse
balloons	coins	hand mirror	ribbon
bar of soap	computer	hand puppets	rubber chicken
barrette	computer diskette	handkerchief	salt and pepper shakers
baseball bat	costume jewelry	hat	scarf
baseball cap	crayons	key chain	scissors
baseball glove	credit card	keys	shoe
basket	crowbar	knitting needle	shoelace
basketball	cup	Koosh Ball	soda can
belt	dental floss	lamp shade	stethoscope
bird's nest	dentist's drill	library card	straw
book	dictionary	light bulb	stuffed animal
bookends	drinking straw	lottery ticket	tambourine
boom box	driver's license	magazine	tape measure
boot	dustpan	marble	telephone
bottle of perfume	earmuffs	marionette	thermometer
Brazil nut	egg	masks	toothbrush
briefcase	electric drill	measuring cup	top hat
bubble gum	encyclopedia	metal file	umbrella
bud vase	envelope	mixing bowl	veil
button	eraser	model airplane	wire hanger
candle	eyeglasses	monkey wrench	yardstick
candy bar	fake mustache	nail file	
candy dish	feather duster	napkins	
cassette tape	felt marker	*The National Enquirer*	
CD	flashlight	Nerf Ball	
cellophane tape	fork	newspaper	
chalkboard eraser	fountain pen	paddle	
chewing gum	frying pan	paper bag	
cigar box	glass	paper clip	
clipboard	glass jar	paper cups	

SPACE PREP
3
MINUTES

PLAYER PREP
30
MINUTES

PERFORMANCE
3
MINUTES

Use These For:

Energy Expender

Group Skills

Icebreaker

PLAYERS
5

Sponge

Teach and Practice:

Blocking and Conventions

Characterization

Concentration

Creativity

Ensemble Acting

Following Directions

Group Dynamics

Listening and Silence

Memorization

Non-vocal Communication

Observation

Physical Control

Plot Structure

Spontaneity

EQUIPMENT
CDs or tapes of "story" music; a CD or tape player for each team; one hand puppet per player.

Puppet Choreography

Directions:
- Divide into teams of five.
- Each team is given or selects a song from the available music. Each team receives a tape or CD player.
- Each player is given or selects a simple hand puppet.
- The teams make up puppet dances using the plot and rhythm of their music. The teams must incorporate a variety of movement including: spacing, rhythm, on/off, up/down, side-to-side, etc.

Example
- *"Monster Mash:"* Puppets may play a scientist, a monster, and a chorus.
- *"Attack of the Killer Tomatoes:"* Puppets may be killer tomatoes, villagers, and/or narrators.

Side Coaching
- Make use of emphasized words in your movement: *"jolt* from my electrode!"
- Avoid lines!
- Vary the positions of your puppets!

Evaluation/Critique
- Was the story communicated?
- Did you know who each puppet represented?
- Was there variety in spacing?
- Were the groupings creative?
- Was there movement to the beat?
- Was it entertaining?
- Did the puppets move (fist puppets) or lip sync (mouth puppets) appropriately?

Challenges and Refinements
- Incorporate musical numbers into a puppet script written by the players.
- Improvise musical numbers to create an opera or rock opera.

Puppet Choreography Music

File name on CD: PCM

"A Wonderful Guy"

"The Addams Family"

"Aquarius"

"All I Want for Christmas"

"All That Jazz"

"Another Opening, Another Show"

"Anything Goes"

"Attack of the Killer Tomatoes"

"Blow, Gabriel, Blow"

"Brush Up Your Shakespeare"

"Camp Granada"

"Do Re Mi"

"Eat It"

"Fish Heads"

"Get a Job"

"Getting to Know You"

"Ghostbusters"

"Go Into Your Dance"

"Grandma Got Run Over by a Reindeer"

"Greased Lightning"

"Happy Talk"

"It's the Hard Knock Life"

"Heaven Hop"

"Hello Dolly"

"Hey, Rickie"

"I Get Around"

"I Love Paris"

"I Saw Mommy Kissing Santa Claus"

"I'd Do Anything"

"Nuttin' for Christmas"

"If You Could See Her"

"June Is Busting Out All Over"

"Kids"

"King Tut"

"Lasagna"

"Leader of the Pack"

"Like a Surgeon"

"Little Deuce Coupe"

"Little Shop of Horrors"

"The Lonely Goatherd"

"Low Rider"

"The Lusty Month of May"

"Matchmaker"

"Monster Mash"

"My Favorite Things"

"There's No Business Like Show Business"

"Peanut Butter"

"Phony Calls"

"You've Got to Pick a Pocket or Two"

"Poisoning Pigeons in the Park"

"The Purple People Eater"

"Put On a Happy Face"

"So Long, Farewell"

"Springtime for Hitler"

"Summer Nights"

"Surfin' Bird"

"The Telephone Hour"

"Youth of the Nation"

"There is Nothing Like a Dame"

"They're Coming to Take Me Away"

"Time Warp"

"Too Darn Hot"

"I'm Gonna Wash That Man Right Outta My Hair"

"We Go Together"

"With a Little Bit o'Luck"

"Yackety Yack"

"Itsie, Bitsie, Teeny, Weeny, Yellow Polka-Dot Bikini"

"Yoda"

"Dentist!"

"You're the Top"

SPACE PREP	PLAYER PREP	PERFORMANCE
0	**3**	**<5**
MINUTES	MINUTES	MINUTES

Use These For:

Energy Expender

Group Skills

Icebreaker

Sponge

PLAYERS
4-5

Teach and Practice:

Blocking and Conventions

Characterization

Concentration

Creativity

Ensemble Acting

Following Directions

Group Dynamics

Listening and Silence

Memorization

Non-vocal Communication

Observation

Physical Control

Plot Structure

Spontaneity

EQUIPMENT

None.

Party Quirk Endowments

Directions

- Divide into teams of four to five. One player is chosen to be the host of a party. Three or four other players are chosen to be guests.
- The host leaves the room.
- Each one of the guests is endowed with a quirk. This may be drawn from a box or assigned by the group or director while the host is out of earshot. (Note: Usually the rest of the group is aware of the endowments.)
- The host starts the party. As each guest arrives s/he plays his/her quirk as a natural part of his/her personality.
- The host gradually amasses enough information during the course of the party to guess each guest's quirk.
- When the host guesses, he or she acknowledges the quirk as part of the scene and continues to guess the rest.

Side Coaching

- Play your quirk, but don't make it totally obvious!
- Anthropomorphize your quirk if it is not human!
- If you are the host, try not to guess unless you are fairly certain! This is not "Twenty Questions"!
- Guests may return to the group when they have been guessed correctly!
- The audience should avoid shouting out clues!

Evaluation/Critique

- Was the guest able to play the quirk without giving it away?
- How did the guest incorporate the quirk into his personality?
- What clues were useful to the host?
- Were the guests able to have a reasonably normal party scene with the incorporation of the quirks?

constant memory lapses

deranged war veteran

drill sergeant

feels persecuted

has to go to the bathroom and doesn't
    want to tell anyone

hates cheese

hates the host

hypnotist

hypochondria

in a hurry

itching

James Bond

killer bee

kleptomaniac

lost child looking for parent

masochist

member of a boy band

Mr. Fix-It

multiple personalities

narcissist

narcolepsy

president

retired kindergarten teacher

Richard Simmons

robber

sadist

scientist

secretly loves the host

shoplifter with the goods

ski bum

stalker

superhero

supermodel

tattoo artist

terrified of bugs

terrified of loud noises

terrorist

undercover FBI agent

vegetarian convert

ventriloquist who has lost his dummy

waiting to be discovered

works hunting sheep

worried about body odor

zombie

What

SPACE PREP	PLAYER PREP	PERFORMANCE
0	**0**	**1-3**
MINUTES	MINUTES	MINUTES

Use These For:

Energy Expender

Group Skills

Icebreaker

Sponge

PLAYERS 2

Teach and Practice:

Blocking and Conventions

Characterization

Concentration

Creativity

Ensemble Acting

Following Directions

Group Dynamics

Listening and Silence

Memorization

Non-vocal Communication

Observation

Physical Control

Plot Structure

Spontaneity

EQUIPMENT
None.

We Don't See Eye-to-Eye

Directions

- Divide into teams of two.
- Each player thinks of, draws, or is assigned a reason, want, or motivation.
- The audience may suggest a *Time* (page 157) and *Place* (page 119).
- The players have one to three minutes to act out a scene in which their reasons, wants, and/or motivations are in conflict.
- The scene must have a beginning, a middle, and an end. The scene must develop the conflict into a crisis and then resolve it.

Evaluation/Critique

- Did the players have individual characters?
- Did the plot have a beginning, a middle, and an end?
- Was there dramatic tension due to the conflict?
- Was the conflict resolved?

Reasons/Wants/Motivations

File name on CD: RWM

to ace the test

to be different

to be noticed

to be popular

to be respected

to be strong

to be successful

to be the same

to be well-liked

to blend in

to break free

Prom-posal competition

to breathe freely

to bring harmony to the situation

to cause trouble

to conquer the world

to escape

to fall in love

to find the hidden treasure

to find what's lost

to find your way out of the woods

to finish the problem

to fix a problem

to get a drink of water

to get a good grade on the test

to get away with something

to get invited to the dance

to get permission

to get recognition

to get respect

to get the girl/boy

to get well

to go to the bathroom

to grow stronger

to guess the answer

to have a boyfriend/girlfriend

to hurt

to know the answer

to learn to drive

to mediate a conflict

to not be afraid

to outsmart the enemy

to overcome depression

to overcome the bully

to rescue the damsel

to thwart the villain

to understand the meaning of life

SPACE PREP
2
MINUTES

PLAYER PREP
2
MINUTES

PERFORMANCE
10
MINUTES

Death in a Restaurant

Use These For:

Energy Expender

Group Skills

Icebreaker

Sponge

PLAYERS
6

Teach and Practice:

Blocking and Conventions

Characterization

Concentration

Creativity

Ensemble Acting

Following Directions

Group Dynamics

Listening and Silence

Memorization

Non-vocal Communication

Observation

Physical Control

Plot Structure

Spontaneity

EQUIPMENT
6 chairs, 3 tables or stools.

Directions

- Divide into teams of six. Teams divide into three pairs of players. Pairs are numbered 1, 2, and 3.
- The players think of, draw, or are assigned a type of restaurant.
- Each pair chooses a *Relationship* (page 151; e.g. mother/daughter, friends) and/or situation (*Scenes for Adjectives* on page 13 gives ideas that may be the situation at the restaurant or before or after the meal, e.g. birthday celebration, prom, etc.).
- Each pair sits at a table (or stool) opposite each other.
- The director whispers "yes" or "no" to each player. The players who are told "yes" find a *motivation* for dying in the scene. They may *not* reveal this to anyone.
- The director calls a pair's number. That pair starts a conversation that reflects their relationship or situation.
- The director calls another pair's number. At this point the performing pair freezes exactly where they are, and the pair called starts a conversation.
- The director continues calling numbers at intervals with the performing pairs stopping *exactly* when another number is called and the called pair starting *precisely* where they left off.

Example

In a sushi restaurant, one player reveals that he has an allergy to a type of fish. The other players/audience believe that he will use that as a motivation for dying, but actually he orders correctly (he was not chosen to die) and is fine. The player who was slated to die ends up choking on something in her sushi.

Side Coaching

- Play your characters!
- Make sure the relationship between you is obvious!
- Use the relationship to develop conflict/move the plot along!
- You may throw in a red herring (false clue) or foreshadowing!
- Do *not* die too soon!
- Make your death motivated!

Evaluation/Critique

- Did the various players foreshadow their deaths? How? Was it necessary?
- Were the deaths motivated?
- Did the various players interact with each other?

Challenges and Refinements

- This game can be played with the pairs able to react to the other players, even though only one pair speaks at a time. This adds more material for motivations and also makes the scene more "believable," as normal people would comment on bodies dropping beside them.
- A waiter who does not freeze may also be used. This works particularly well with beginners. The waiter could be the director.

Playing Option

This may be played with only one pair, omitting the freezes.

Restaurants

American
Bar and Grill
Barbecue
Buffet
Cajun
Cantonese Chinese
Chinese
Coffee Shop
Continental
Cyber Cafe
Deli
Drive-In
Fast Food
French
German
Greasy Spoon
Greek
Ice Cream Parlor
Indian (east)
Italian
Italian-American
Japanese
Jewish
Korean
Mediterranean
Mexican
Middle Eastern
Mongolian
Native American
Natural Foods
New Mexican
Pancake House
Pastry Shop
Pizza
Sandwich
Seafood
Southwestern
Spanish
Steak House
Sushi
Szechuan
Thai
Vegetarian
Vietnamese
Wine Bar

Ways to Die in a Restaurant
File name on CD: WDR

Allergic reaction

Attacked by ex-spouse

Ceiling fan falls and minces diner

Ceiling fans

Choke on food

Cut by a knife

Die of fright

Drive-by shooting

Drown in soup

Fall and hit head

Fatal nose bleed

Food poisoning

Heart attack at menu prices

Knocked down by a waiter

Shock at a bill

Shot in a holdup

Stabbed with a fork

Stabbed with a knife

Trampled by an extra large family

Tripped on a rug

Players will have even *more* creative ideas!

Use These For:

Energy Expender

Group Skills

Icebreaker

Sponge

PLAYERS
4-6

Teach and Practice:

Blocking and Conventions

Characterization

Concentration

Creativity

Ensemble Acting

Following Directions

Group Dynamics

Listening and Silence

Memorization

Non-vocal Communication

Observation

Physical Control

Plot Structure

Spontaneity

EQUIPMENT
Assorted tables, chairs, and props as available and needed.

CSI: Your Hometown

Directions

- Divide into teams of four to six.
- Each team draws a room, a crime or imaginary crime, and a weapon.
- Given these three starters, each team develops a scene about their crime. The scene may show the crime, the aftermath of the crime, or a detective discovering and solving the crime.
- Scenes should be about five minutes long and should have a complete plot with a beginning, a middle, and an ending.

Example

- A *burglary* in the *bedroom* with a *computer*. The scene revolves around a group of teenage girls at a sleepover using the hostess's computer to hack into the local high school to change (steal) their grades.
- The imaginary crime of *wearing Birkenstocks* in the *living room* with a *gun*. The scene revolves around a formal party at a home. When the host family's daughter's boyfriend arrives in Birkenstocks, the father takes out a gun and threatens him until he agrees to leave and come back wearing more appropriate footwear.

Evaluation/Critique

- Was the crime logically incorporated into the scene?
- Was the weapon used? Was the weapon used to commit the crime or contribute to its resolution?
- Were the characters useful to the plot?

Challenges and Refinements

- Teams first draw only the crime. The crime is set up before the weapon prompt is drawn.
- Choose an outside improviser to enter the scene as a detective after the crime has been committed.
- Use this as a straight improv with no prep time.
- Add types of characters, attitudes, accents, etc.
- Have six teams, each showing a different aspect of the crime.
  Example:
  - Team 1: Foreshadowing.
  - Team 2: The commission of the crime.
  - Team 3: The perpetrator's escape.
  - Team 4: The discovery of the crime.
  - Team 5: Discovering the essential clue.
  - Team 6: The resolution.

Rooms in a House

File name on CD: Rooms

attic

aviary

back hall

back porch

balcony

ballroom

basement

bathroom

bedroom

billiard room

boudoir

breakfast nook

broom closet

butler's pantry

carport

cellar

closet

conservatory

corridor

deck

den

dining room

drawing room

dressing room

entry hall

family room

formal dining room

front hall

front porch

gallery

game room

garage

garret

great room

greenhouse

gym

kennel

kitchen

laundry room

living room

lounge

master bedroom

morning room

mother-in-law's quarters

mud room

music room

nursery

office

pantry

parlor

passage

playroom

porch

recreation room

reception hall

rumpus room

sauna

servant's quarters

sewing room

sitting room

solarium

spa

stoop

studio

terrace

TV room

veranda

walk-in closet

workshop

Crimes

Real Crimes

abduction
adultery
animal abuse
arson
assault
bail jumping
bank robbery
battery
blackmail
bomb threats
bombing
bribery
burglary
carrying a concealed weapon
child abuse
contributing to the delinquency
  of a minor
credit card fraud
date rape
defacing public property
disappearance
dognapping
drive-by shooting
driving while intoxicated
drug abuse
drug growing
drug possession
drug trafficking
drunk and disorderly behavior
embezzlement
extortion
failure to appear
fencing
forgery
fraud
graffiti
grand theft auto
harassment
hit and run
identity theft
incest
inhalant abuse
insider trading
intellectual property piracy
jail breaking
kidnapping
larceny
loitering

maiming
manslaughter
money laundering
mugging
murder
neglect
negligent use of firearms
perjury
plagiarism
poaching
possession of explosives
prostitution
rape
receiving stolen property
robbery
running away
sexual assault
sexual harassment
shoplifting
shrinkage
slander
slave trading
software piracy
solicitation
soliciting a prostitute
spotlighting
terrorism
theft
threatening phone calls
transporting minors across state
  lines for immoral purposes
treason
vandalism
violating curfew
violation of probation
writing bad checks

Imaginary Crimes

Altoid abuse
arrogance
bad fashion sense
bad manners
bad odor
bad taste
being a ditz
being a know-it-all
being a twit
belching
blowing nose in public

bullying
bullying on the playground
causing wedgies
cow tipping
dirty dancing
driving a beater
driving over the age of 55
eating granola
eating too fast
enjoying math
gum chewing in public
lying
making prank phone calls
making puns
misspelling
nail biting
name calling
nickname calling
nose picking
not balancing your checkbook
not doing homework
overeating
painting nails in public
pie throwing
prank calling
quoting out of context
reading all the time
rudeness
sagging
scratching
skateboarding
slouching
smiling too much
sneezing loudly
spilling food on your clothes
squeaky voice
talking too much
telling dumb jokes
too many piercings
too many tattoos
Tums abuse
ugly hair dying
ugly tattoos
wearing Birkenstocks

Murder Weapons

File name on CD: Weapons

abandoned refrigerator

acid

air rifle

anthrax

arrow

assault weapon

attack dog

automobile

ax

bandanna

BB gun

black widow spider

blowtorch

board with nail

boiling oil

bomb

brick

brown recluse spider

butcher knife

carbon monoxide poisoning

computer

crowbar

curare

curtain cord

duct tape

electric garage door

electrical cord

exploding staircase

explosives

fire

fireworks

fishing knife

fishing line

flashlight

frozen mackerel

frying pan

garrote

glass cutter

gold paint

hair dryer in bathtub

hatchet

iron

jump rope

kerosene

knitting needle

laser pointer

lawn tractor

lead pipe

leg of lamb

machete

man-eating plant

meat cleaver

microwave oven

mirror

nail file

paintball gun

paper cutter

piranha

plastic explosives

poisoned chocolate

poisoned dart

poisoned drink

poison gas

poisoned injection

poisoned medication

poisoned popcorn

poisonous snake

rat poison

revolver

rifle

rope

samurai sword

Saturday night special

scalding water

scorpion

shark

shotgun

statue

swimming pool

Swiss army knife

switchblade

telephone cord

telephone receiver

truck

Uzi

wild animal

zip gun

Who

SPACE PREP
0
MINUTES

PLAYER PREP
0
MINUTES

PERFORMANCE
2
MINUTES

Use These For:

Energy Expender

Group Skills

Icebreaker

Sponge

PLAYERS
2

Teach and Practice:

Blocking and Conventions

Characterization

Concentration

Creativity

Ensemble Acting

Following Directions

Group Dynamics

Listening and Silence

Memorization

Non-vocal Communication

Observation

Physical Control

Plot Structure

Spontaneity

EQUIPMENT
None.

You've Got a Secret

Directions

- Divide into teams of two. Teams divide into As and Bs.
- Player A is told a secret about player B and vice versa.
- A *Generic Scene* (page 71) starts in which each player knows a secret about the other.
- The scene progresses as each player reacts to the other as if this secret is an important part of the other player.
- Players should eventually guess their own secrets.
- *Or*, players have secrets that affect their actions in the scene. The players try to guess each other's secret.

Example

- The Breakup: Player A is told that Player B has a *fake Ph.D*. B is told that A has *just gotten out of prison*. Both of them focus on deception and how the other has not been honest. That is the major reason for the breakup.
- The Breakup (alternate play): Player A has a *fake Ph.D*. Player B has had a *face-lift*. Player A wants to break the news to B easily while B feels that her face-lift should make A want to stay with her.

Evaluation/Critique

- Did the players try to reveal the secrets by showing, not telling?
- Did the secret further the action?

I am afraid of _____.

I am afraid of cats.

I am afraid of dogs.

I am afraid of enclosed spaces.

I am afraid of heights.

I am afraid of lightning.

I am afraid of little kids.

I am afraid of loud noises.

I am afraid of snakes.

I am afraid of spiders.

I am afraid of the color black.

I am afraid of the number 13.

I am allergic to air.

I am allergic to boys.

I am allergic to chocolate.

I am allergic to girls.

I am allergic to light.

I am allergic to notebook paper.

I am allergic to television.

I am attracted to the color _____.

I am compulsive about combing my hair.

I am compulsive about making my bed.

I am compulsive about setting the table.

I am compulsive about tying my shoes.

I am compulsive about wearing blue eye shadow.

I am really a man/woman.

I am secretly attracted to bugs.

I am secretly attracted to dogs.

I am secretly attracted to money.

I am secretly attracted to people with black hair.

I am secretly attracted to the word "no."

I am secretly attracted to you.

I am wearing a toupee.

I bite my nails.

I didn't graduate from high school.

I hate people who wear blue.

I hate people with brown eyes.

I hate the word _____.

I have a fake Ph.D.

I have a fatal disease.

I have chronic bad breath.

I have had a face-lift.

I have smelly feet.

I just got out of prison.

I made up my name.

I will do anything for money.

I'm not really a doctor.

I'm older than I look.

I'm underage.

My clothes are on backwards.

My pride and joy is _____.

People who bite their nails disgust me.

People who have acne disgust me.

People who have pierced ears disgust me.

People who wear jeans disgust me.

There's someone else.

When I get nervous I belch.

When I get nervous I choke.

When I get nervous I cough.

When I get nervous I faint.

When I get nervous I fidget.

When I get nervous I have seizures.

When I get nervous I lose my voice.

When I get nervous I scream.

Who

SPACE PREP	PLAYER PREP	PERFORMANCE
0	**2**	**~**
MINUTES	MINUTES	MINUTES

Use These For:

Energy Expender

Group Skills

Icebreaker

PLAYERS
Full Group

Sponge

Teach and Practice:

Blocking and Conventions

Characterization

Concentration

Creativity

Ensemble Acting

Following Directions

Group Dynamics

Listening and Silence

Memorization

Non-vocal Communication

Observation

Physical Control

Plot Structure

Spontaneity

EQUIPMENT

None.

Sensing

Directions

- Each member of the group finds a spot on the floor, or pairs sit in a circle with backs to each other.
- The director turns off all lights and ambient sounds in the room if possible.
- The players close their eyes.
- The director creates a scenario to which the players react using their senses. The director may concentrate on one sensory category or choose a few from each.
- The director asks each player to react non-vocally to the stated sensory stimuli. Players should try to use their entire bodies while reacting.

Example

- Auditory only: You have just entered a crowded restaurant where you've never been before. You have just been seated when you hear a *crash* (pause), followed by a *wail* (pause). You hear a *moan* behind you (pause). The moan turns into a *whimper* (pause).
- All five senses: For your birthday you have gotten a big box tied with a bow. It is *gigantic* (pause). You shake it and hear a *soft thud* (pause). You smell a *musty odor* (pause). Opening it, you pull out a *lumpy* object that appears to be some sort of *tropical fruit* (pause). Gingerly you put a piece of it on the tip of your *tongue* (pause). It tastes *sour yet spicy* (pause).

Sensory Stimuli

File name on CD:
Stimuli

Auditory (hearing)	Olfactory (smell)	Optical (seeing)	Tactile (touch)	Taste
applause	acrid	alien	bumpy	acrid
bang	aromatic	beautiful	cold	bitter
crack	astringent	brilliant	cool	bland
crash	bitter	clean	cuddly	chalky
cry	burning	clear	dry	creamy
groan	caustic	colorful	dusty	crumbly
growl	chemical	cute	elastic	crunchy
grunt	citrus	dismal	filthy	delicious
harmonic	dank	dull	fluffy	dry
high-pitched	dusty	fancy	frosty	fruity
hiss	floral	fat	gooey	hot
howl	foul	filthy	greasy	medicinal
loud	fragrant	fluffy	hairy	nutty
mechanical	fruity	gigantic	icy	peppery
melodic	harsh	glamorous	light	rotten
moan	medicinal	grotesque	lumpy	salty
musical	musky	homely	moist	savory
pop	musty	human	prickly	sharp
repetitive	noxious	immense	rough	slimy
roar	pungent	large	round	smoky
rumble	putrid	little	sharp	smooth
scream	rotten	minuscule	silky	soggy
screech	salty	murky	slimy	sour
sharp	savory	ordinary	slippery	spicy
shushing	sharp	plain	smooth	stale
single tone	smoky	round	soft	sweet
snarl	spicy	shadowy	springy	tangy
soft	stale	sharp		tart
thud	sweaty	short		yeasty
wail	sweet	small		
whimper		smooth		
whinny		solid		
whistle		tall		
windy		thin		
yip		tiny		
		ugly		
		unusual		

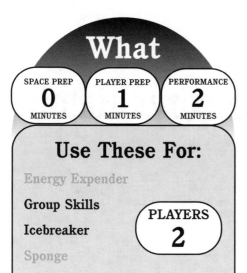

SPACE PREP
0
MINUTES

PLAYER PREP
1
MINUTES

PERFORMANCE
2
MINUTES

Use These For:

Energy Expender

Group Skills

Icebreaker

Sponge

PLAYERS
2

Teach and Practice:

Blocking and Conventions

Characterization

Concentration

Creativity

Ensemble Acting

Following Directions

Group Dynamics

Listening and Silence

Memorization

Non-vocal Communication

Observation

Physical Control

Plot Structure

Spontaneity

EQUIPMENT
None.

Scenes in Slang

Directions
- Divide into teams of two.
- A list of slang (current and passé) is handed to each player.
- Each pair of players decides on the who, where, and what of the scene. (Example: Two friends on a beach checking out the opposite gender.)
- Players improvise a scene with a beginning, middle, and end in which they use no dialogue but the provided slang.

Side Coaching
- Establish who, where, and what right away!
- Develop at least one conflict!
- Use your entire vocal range to add variety to the slang!
- You may repeat slang expressions for emphasis!

Challenges and Refinements
- Limit the amount of slang.
- See if the pairs can prepare a one-minute scene using no more than five expressions.

Evaluation/Critique
- Were you able to understand the plot when only a limited number of words/expressions were used?
- Did vocal variety make a difference?

Challenges and Refinements
- Try using the American Film Institute's top 100 movie songs or film titles instead of slang.
- Use any interesting list of your own in the same way.

a'ight

ain't

all that

as if

awesome

bad

bangin'

be real

BF

biter

bling

bling bling

blows

bodacious

bounce

BRB

busted

cheddar

chick

chill

chillin'

chillin' like a villain

clean up good

cold

coner

cool

crib

da bomb

daddy-o

dank

dawg

deaded

dime out

dog

dope

dope out

dork

down with that

dude

dweeb

eww

excellent

far out

fess up

fine

floss

for real

for sure

freaky

funky

FYI

get down with it

get medieval

GF

ghetto

ghetto booty

girlfriend

gnarley

grip

groovy

hang loose

hater

hella

hey, bro

homie

hoser

hot

hottie

ice

it's a trip

jacked

janky

jiggy

juiced

keen

keep it real

kickin'

kill it

lame

last year

later

later days

laterz

lit

LOL

mack

mad

mean

mondo bizarro

money

my bad

nasty

neat-o

not

off the hook

oh, you kid

peace out

peachy

phat

poser

punk

punked

rad

random

raunchy

ride

riding high

right on

rock on

ROTFL

sad

shoot the breeze

sick

slick

spiffy

step off

straight up

sucks

sup

super

sweet

the cat's meow

this blows

this rocks

this sucks

tight

time out

TMI

toast

toasted

tool

torqued

totally

trip

trip out

trippin'

tubular

twenty-three skidoo

wack

wassup

wasted

weak

what's poppin'

whatever

wicked

word

word up

wuss

yadda, yadda, yadda

yeah, right

yo

you da bomb

you go

you go, girl

you rock

your mama

your mom

your mother

yow

yowsers

yowzah

yup

zoned

zonked

What

SPACE PREP
0
MINUTES

PLAYER PREP
0
MINUTES

PERFORMANCE
~
MINUTES

Use These For:

Energy Expender

Group Skills

Icebreaker

Sponge

PLAYERS
2

Teach and Practice:

Blocking and Conventions

Characterization

Concentration

Creativity

Ensemble Acting

Following Directions

Group Dynamics

Listening and Silence

Memorization

Non-vocal Communication

Observation

Physical Control

Plot Structure

Spontaneity

EQUIPMENT

Optional — piano or keyboard.

Musical Improv

Directions

- Divide into teams of two.
- Divide the playing space into four areas. Each area represents a different song style.
- The audience suggests a scene title.
- The players start the scene in one area, eventually breaking into the song style of the area.
- They sing — in the appropriate style — in each performance area.

Example

Home Again! The players start in the opera area and sing a duet about starting their married life in their new house. They move into the romantic area and sing about how much they love each other and are hopeful of the future. They then move to the country area and sing about the financial problems that may hold them back. They end in the torch song area where they realize that they can't afford the house and decide to divorce.

Evaluation/Critique

- Were the transitions clear?
- Did the dialogue lead up to the song?
- Did the style of song fit the mood of the scene?

Challenges and Refinements

- If the group has a pianist who can improvise, the players may make up songs in different styles played by the pianist.
- A certain style may be played and a line of four players may add stanzas one at a time.

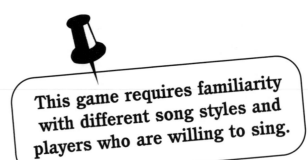

This game requires familiarity with different song styles and players who are willing to sing.

Song Styles

ambient	Gregorian chant	patriotic
art song	hard rock	polka
baroque	Hawaiian	pop
bluegrass	hip-hop	progressive rock
blues	hoedown	punk
Celtic	hymns	rap
Celtic rock	inspirational	rhythm and blues
classical	Irish drinking	rock and roll
country and western	jazz	rockabilly
cowboy	Latin	romantic
disco	lounge	salsa
easy listening	marching songs	soul
elevator	Mariachi	spiritual
folk	musical comedy	swing
folk rock	oompah-pah	techno
gospel	opera	torch song

SPACE PREP
5
MINUTES

PLAYER PREP
5
MINUTES

PERFORMANCE
3
MINUTES

Use These For:

Energy Expender

Group Skills

Icebreaker

Sponge

PLAYERS
5

Teach and Practice:

Blocking and Conventions

Characterization

Concentration

Creativity

Ensemble Acting

Following Directions

Group Dynamics

Listening and Silence

Memorization

Non-vocal Communication

Observation

Physical Control

Plot Structure

Spontaneity

EQUIPMENT
Microphones (or other method of amplifying voices); screen, curtains, or flats to conceal performers.

Suspense

Directions

- Divide into teams of five.
- Each team draws six to ten sound effects.
- The teams get five minutes to plan a suspenseful radio drama using only their voices to create the dialogue and sound effects.
- The radio drama should be amplified and performed out of sight of the audience if possible.
- The radio drama should be no longer than three minutes and must create suspense.

Example

Using an *airplane takeoff, baby crying, ambulance siren, rain,* and *screaming,* the team acts out the story of an airplane that comes to a very rocky landing, injuring several passengers including a baby.

Evaluation/Critique

- Was it possible to use just voices to create sound effects?
- Which sound effects were most effective?
- Did the sound effects contribute to the overall mood?
- Did the sound effects contribute to the suspense?

Challenges and Refinements

Use prerecorded sound effects and incorporate these into a written script.

Sound Effects

airplane takeoff

ambulance siren

applause

baby crying

baby laughing

battle

bears growling

birds chirping

blizzard

bomb

bomb explosion

breaking glass

car alarm

car chase

car crash

car horn

chairs scraping

church clock striking

clock ticking

cork popping

crowd cheering

crowd running

door closing

door creaking

door opening

door slamming

doorbell chime

drum patterns

dynamite explosion

fire engines

firecrackers

fireworks

foghorn

footsteps running

galloping horses

glass breaking

grandfather clock

gunfight

heartbeat

heavy breathing

horse neigh

knife being sharpened

laughing

laughter and clapping

lion roar

machine gun fire

man screaming

moans

monster coming to life

New York subway

owl hooting

pedestrians on city streets

phone ringing

physical exertion

pinball machine

police sirens

pots and pans

rain

rapid door knocks

reveille

rocket launch

screaming

seagulls

series of explosions

sink draining

snoring

swarm of bees

taps

telephone busy signal

telephone ringing

thunder

tires screeching

toilet flushing

tower clock

water dripping

water running

whimpering

wolves howling

wooden gate creaking

SPACE PREP
0
MINUTES

PLAYER PREP
0
MINUTES

PERFORMANCE
6
MINUTES

SPAR (Spontaneous Argumentation)

Use These For:

Energy Expender

Group Skills

Icebreaker

Sponge

PLAYERS
2

Teach and Practice:

Blocking and Conventions

Characterization

Concentration

Creativity

Ensemble Acting

Following Directions

Group Dynamics

Listening and Silence

Memorization

Non-vocal Communication

Observation

Physical Control

Plot Structure

Spontaneity

EQUIPMENT
None.

Directions

- Choose two players to SPAR. Players come to the front of the group and are assigned affirmative (pro) or negative (con) sides.
- Players are given a resolution (topic).
- The pro player gets one minute to state his or her opening arguments.
- The con player gets one minute to state his or her opening arguments.
- The pro player gets one minute to rebut the con player's opening arguments.
- The con player gets one minute to rebut the pro player's opening arguments.
- The pro player gets one minute to make a closing statement.
- The con player gets one minute to make a closing statement.
- The rest of the group critiques.

Hints for Success

- What makes a good argument? (See *Persuasion and Propaganda Techniques* in Appendix 3 on page 193.)
- How do you convince someone that you are correct?

Example

Tall people are superior to short people.

Pro ideas: Scientists have shown that a person's height is directly related to his or her future income (make up statistics or studies).

Con ideas: Judging people's superiority by body size is irrelevant. Look at Napoleon. And how do you define superior, anyway?

Evaluation/Critique

- Ridiculous arguments and fake facts can be used but must be effective, not random.
- What doesn't work: accusations, anger, repetition, etc.

Challenges and Refinements

- Stress logic.
- This can be used as a simple icebreaker just for fun. The more ridiculous the topic, the better. (Example: dogs are better pets than cats.)
- Use this as pre-debate training allowing for minimal research and limited sources.

All Americans should be required to learn Spanish as well as English.

All guns should be confiscated and melted down for scrap metal.

All religious holidays should be celebrated.

All students should be trilingual.

Backpacks should not be allowed in school.

Blondes are smarter than brunettes.

Blue-eyed people are nicer than brown-eyed people.

Brides should wear red rather than white.

Country music should be banned.

Dogs are better pets than cats.

Drama should be required of all students.

English should be the only language in the United States.

Every high school graduate should be required to serve in the military for two years after graduation.

Everyone over the age of seventy should be euthanized.

Everyone over the age of sixteen should be required to carry a gun.

Everyone should be a vegetarian.

Everyone should be required to pass a swimming test in order to graduate from high school.

Everyone should be required to play a musical instrument in order to graduate from high school.

Everyone should be required to wear long pants.

Everyone should be required to work out one hour a day.

Fingernail biting should be punished with a year in jail.

Girls are superior to boys.

If a tree falls in a forest and no human hears it, it does not make a sound.

No one may eat more than 1,500 calories a day.

No one may make over $75,000 a year.

No one should be allowed to have more than one child.

No one should be allowed to watch TV on a school night.

No one should be allowed to wear makeup.

No one should be required to say the Lord's Prayer.

No religious holiday may be celebrated.

Our town does not need a movie theatre.

Red is a better color than black.

Smoking should be banned everywhere.

Tall people are superior to short people.

The chicken came before the egg.

The drinking age should be lowered to sixteen.

The government must provide universal health care.

The U.S. national anthem should be changed to "America the Beautiful."

There should be a ten o'clock curfew for everyone under eighteen years of age.

There should be a universal school dress code.

There should be no homework.

TV cartoons inspire violent behavior.

We should be allowed to wear hats in school.

We should do away with the movie/TV rating system.

We should have block scheduling in all secondary schools.

We should have only single-sex schools.

We should have school uniforms.

We should have year-round school.

Winnie the Pooh should be our school mascot.

SPACE PREP
0
MINUTES

PLAYER PREP
5
MINUTES

PERFORMANCE
3
MINUTES

Use These For:

Energy Expender

Group Skills

Icebreaker

Sponge

PLAYERS
2

Teach and Practice:

Blocking and Conventions

Characterization

Concentration

Creativity

Ensemble Acting

Following Directions

Group Dynamics

Listening and Silence

Memorization

Non-vocal Communication

Observation

Physical Control

Plot Structure

Spontaneity

EQUIPMENT
None.

Status Slide

Directions

- Divide into teams of two.
- Each pair draws or is assigned a relationship. Each relationship has a traditionally higher-status person and a traditionally lower-status person (master/servant).
- Each pair plans a scene in which the players emphasize their expected relationships. The higher status player always puts the lower status player down and raises himself. The lower status player should lower himself while raising the higher status player.
- Each pair performs for the group.
- At some time during the action, the director calls out, "switch!"
- Although the players keep their same characters, they must slowly switch status until both are completely opposite from the way they started.

Example

Doctor/patient. The doctor tells the patient that all her medical problems are caused by her obesity. The patient is in agony, agreeing that she has no control over her appetite. When they switch, the patient becomes enraged at the doctor's patronizing attitude toward her problems. She turns the tables on the doctor by pointing out some of his shortcomings. The doctor whiningly agrees.

Side Coaching

- High status characters: Build yourself up while putting the other down!
- Low status characters: Put yourself down by agreeing with the criticisms!

Challenges and Refinements

Play the scene with the traditional high status character being low status and vice versa.

Status Relationships

File name on CD: Relationships

apprentice/master

artist/model

boyfriend/girlfriend

brother/sister

child/adult

clerk/customer

criminal/police

criminal/victim

debtor/lender

devil/angel

director/actor

director/auditioner

doctor/patient

employer/employee

experienced/inexperienced

fan/movie star

good cop/bad cop

good guy/bad guy

good/evil

happy/sad

healthy/unhealthy

husband/wife

in crowd/out crowd

intelligent/unintelligent

king/subject

lawyer/client

leader/follower

lucky/unlucky

male/female

manipulator/puppet

master/servant

parent/child

pet/master

player/coach

politician/constituent

popular/unpopular

psychiatrist/patient

rich person/poor person

slave/master

soldier/civilian

sophisticated/naive

teacher/parent

teacher/student

young/old

SPACE PREP
0
MINUTES

PLAYER PREP
0
MINUTES

PERFORMANCE
2-3
MINUTES

Use These For:

Energy Expender

Group Skills

Icebreaker

Sponge

PLAYERS
2

Teach and Practice:

Blocking and Conventions

Characterization

Concentration

Creativity

Ensemble Acting

Following Directions

Group Dynamics

Listening and Silence

Memorization

Non-vocal Communication

Observation

Physical Control

Plot Structure

Spontaneity

EQUIPMENT
None.

To the Rescue

Directions

- Divide into teams of two.
- The group thinks of a serious crisis.
- Two players are endowed with "super powers."
- The two players play a scene trying to use their "super powers" to avert the crisis.

Examples

- A tidal wave is about to hit the city. *News Broadcaster Lady* relays emergency information to *Urge to Scream Guy* who screams it out the window.
- *Super Plumber* tries ways to shore up the city for the tidal wave while *Ballet Boy* dances his ideas.

Side Coaching

- Make the powers seem natural!
- Be creative with your solutions but keep them within the scope of your super powers!

Evaluation/Critique

- Did the players act out their super powers?
- Did the super powers help solve the crisis?
- Did the two superheroes interact constructively?
- Was a solution to the problem found?

Challenges/Refinements

- Play this game with other superheroes coming into the scene.
- Allow the other players to endow new players with super powers.
- Add a super villain to the scene to hinder the heroes (see page 155 for *Super Villains*).

Superheroes

Established and Mythical Heroes

Achilles

Aquaman

Batman

Belleraphon

Blade

Cyclops

Dr. Xavier

GI Joe

Hercules

Hulk

Human Torch

Perseus

Quailman

Robin

Rogue

Shadow

Soldier and Hero

Captain America

Spawn

Spiderman

Storm

Sub-Mariner

Super Boy

Superman

Theseus

Ulysses

Whistler

Wolverine

Wonder Woman

Xena

X-Men

Very New Heroes

Ballet Lady:	She leaps and spins with limitless power.
Bobsledding Boy:	The master of cold transportation, he arrives and leaves on his mysterious bobsled.
Boomerang Boy:	No matter how someone gets rid of him, he comes back.
Bridge Span Man:	He doesn't need a civil engineer — his body becomes a bridge.
ChessMan:	Strategist of the highest powers.
Crisco Kid:	Very — *very* — slick.
Drill Sergeant:	His fingers can drill holes into anything.
Elastic Man:	He can be bent but not broken and can hold things together.
Hairdresser:	Has magic comb, brush, and curling iron that work on anything.
Invisible Boy:	He's there, watching, listening.
Jumping Jack Guy:	His magical legs can propel him over any obstacle.
Masseuse:	She can massage anything into any other shape with her magical hands.
News Broadcaster Lady:	On-the-spot news is her forte.
Precipitation Kid:	He cries — it rains.
Recycle Rider:	Her bicycle allows her to turn anything into anything else.
Red Shoe Boy:	Has magical red shoes that take him where he wants to go (female version is Dorothy).
Rodeo Guy:	Rides broncos — or anything — and can't get thrown.
Running Man:	He runs faster than anyone and never gets tired.
School Marm Ma'am:	She's prim and proper, but can get information through the thickest skull.
Shakespeare Spouter:	The bard has a quote for every situation.
Short Order:	He cooks up solutions and serves them with a side of fries (and he's not very tall).
Sneaker Man:	His magical shoes allow him to move in complete silence.
Solid Waste-Line:	She wraps her belt around something and it goes straight to the landfill.
Speed Limiter:	A temporal policeman who can make time do what he wants.
Super Plumber:	Can un-jam any jam with his plumber's helper.
Tap-Dancing Man:	He taps with grace and skill, covering amazing distances.
The Electrician:	He's shocking but very precise.
Urge to Scream Guy:	He needs to scream for good.
Wellness Woman:	Her herbal remedies can cure everything but a broken heart.

SPACE PREP
2
MINUTES

PLAYER PREP
0
MINUTES

PERFORMANCE
2-3
MINUTES

Use These For:

Energy Expender

Group Skills

Icebreaker

Sponge

PLAYERS
2

Teach and Practice:

Blocking and Conventions

Characterization

Concentration

Creativity

Ensemble Acting

Following Directions

Group Dynamics

Listening and Silence

Memorization

Non-vocal Communication

Observation

Physical Control

Plot Structure

Spontaneity

EQUIPMENT
Assorted tables, chairs, and props as available and needed.

Bad Guy/Good Guy

Directions

• Divide the group into pairs where one player is A, and the other is B.
• A draws the name of a super villain.
• A and B perform a scene in which the super villain causes a crisis for B.

Examples

• A is *Belching Betty*. B is a friend. They go out for a fancy dinner. Betty belches so violently that they get thrown out.
• A is *Freddy Krueger*. B is a little child. B tries to stay awake as Freddy keeps crawling into the bedroom.

Side Coaching

• Play your villainous qualities!
• React to the villain!
• Find a creative way out of the problem!

Evaluation/Critique

• Did the scene have a beginning, middle, and ending?
• Did the super villain reveal her character gradually or right away?
• Did B react to A?
• Did the super villain create a believable crisis?
• Was the crisis resolved?
• Was the super villain defeated or transformed?

Challenges and Refinements

• Have B draw an *Attitude* (page 11) or *Occupation* (page 105).
• Draw a *Place* as well (page 119).
• Have A be a super villain and B be a *Superhero* (page 153).
• Draw a *Crime* to involve A and B (pages 136).

Super Villains

Established Villains	Disney Villains	Could-Be Villains	
Annihilator	Brom Bones *(The Legend of Sleepy Hollow)*	Belching Betty:	The power of her burps sends opponents flying.
Boris and Natasha	Captain Hook *(Peter Pan)*	Cutsie Girl:	They think she's cute and dumb; she's cute and clever.
Carnage		Daddy's Girl:	She'll draw you in with her sweet charms, but watch out for Daddy — he's mean.
Catwoman	Gantu *(Lilo and Stitch)*		
Clown	Gaston *(Beauty and the Beast)*	Fingernail Man:	They look normal, but his fingernails can transform into any tool he wants.
Coyote	Hades *(Hercules)*		
Crabby Appleton	Jafar *(Aladdin)*	Gossip Girl:	She gets the word out through a secret network — but can you trust it?
Craven			
Doomsday	Klayton *(Tarzan)*	Ladies' Man:	When he turns on the charm, women are helpless.
Dr. Moriarty	Madam Mim *(The Sword and the Stone)*	Loudmouth Lady:	She's loud and, when she puts her lungs to it, can be heard over anything.
Dr. Octopus			
Elmer Fudd	Maleficent *(Sleeping Beauty)*	Macho Man:	What a guy, and he won't let you forget it. In trying to prove himself, he destroys everything in his path.
Freddy Krueger	Queen *(Snow White)*		
Green Goblin	Queen of Hearts *(Alice in Wonderland)*	Noodle Man:	He's thin and bendy.
Jason		Opera Singer:	Her beautiful voice can persuade anyone to do anything.
Joker	Scar *(The Lion King)*	Red Lipstick Girl:	The lips are beautiful, but they enslave anyone they touch.
Lex Luthor	Shere Khan & Kaa *(The Jungle Book)*		
Magneto		Snakeman:	His scaly friends do what he orders.
Mystique	Sheriff of Nottingham, Prince John, Sir Hiss *(Robin Hood)*	Snoring Guy:	His snores are the last thing anyone hears before they go to sleep.
Penguin			
Sabertooth	Stepmother *(Cinderella)*	The Terrible Din:	His gift is sound — and lots of it.
Skeletor	Stromboli, Fox *(Pinocchio)*	Urge to Scream Guy:	It's his effect on others that's dangerous — they just want to scream … and scream … and scream.
Sub-Zero	Ursula *(The Little Mermaid)*		
The Riddler	Yzma *(The Emperor's New Groove)*	Walk into Walls Guy:	He's indestructible; too bad he's so clumsy.
Toad			
Venom			

SPACE PREP	PLAYER PREP	PERFORMANCE
2 MINUTES	**0** MINUTES	**5** MINUTES

Use These For:

Energy Expender

Group Skills

Icebreaker

Sponge

PLAYERS
2-4

Teach and Practice:

Blocking and Conventions

Characterization

Concentration

Creativity

Ensemble Acting

Following Directions

Group Dynamics

Listening and Silence

Memorization

Non-vocal Communication

Observation

Physical Control

Plot Structure

Spontaneity

EQUIPMENT
Assorted tables, chairs, and props as available and needed.

Time Travel

Directions

- Divide into teams of two to four.
- The audience chooses a *Film Title* (page 61) or *Generic Scene* (page 71) for the players to improvise.
- Players start the scene in the present (twenty-first century).
- As the scene progresses, the director calls out a new period, and the players gradually shift to the new period and its requisite style.

Side Coaching

- Make the switch believable!
- Keep your same personality characteristics, but modify them to suit the time!

Example

I Can Fix That. Players start out with a broken dishwasher. Two characters have the dishwasher in pieces on the floor when two neighbors enter with tools and offer to help. They switch to the *Pilgrims at Plymouth Rock.* The "dishwasher" is now a tub with a hole in it. The tools become more primitive, but the attitude of the neighbors is the same — they can do anything. It becomes increasingly obvious that the neighbors' enthusiasm is greater than their skill as they insist that they are experts at fixing anything. At the next switch, *Lindbergh Flies the Atlantic*, the "dishwasher" is a sink and a drain rack. The sink is stopped up, and the same neighbors continue to help ineptly.

Evaluation/Critique

- Do the time period changes seem believable?
- Were the transitions smooth?
- Are the original characters still recognizable?

Challenges and Refinements

- Divide the large group into teams of two to four.
- Give each team a different time period.
- The entire group shows the same scene in different time periods.

The wise leader chooses times that are familiar to the players. Teachers might check with social studies and/or history teachers for periods students know.

●com   http://www.eyewitnesstohistory.com

18,000 BCE: Most recent ice age

10,000 BCE: Neolithic

4,000 BCE: Iron Age

3,300 BCE: Bronze Age

551 BCE: Confucius born

399 BCE: Death of Socrates

333 BCE: Alexander defeats Persians

208 BCE: Great Wall of China (start)

44 BCE: Julius Caesar assassinated

64 CE: Burning of Rome

79 CE: Vesuvius covers Pompeii and Herculaneum

361 CE: Huns in Europe

1066 CE: Norman Invasion of England

1099 CE: Crusaders capture Jerusalem

1347 CE: Black Death in Europe

1492 CE: Columbus arrives in America

1522 CE: Magellan's ships sail around globe

1533 CE: Henry VIII divorces Catherine of Aragon

1587 CE: Execution of Mary, Queen of Scotts

1607 CE: John Smith saved by Pocahontas

1620 CE: Pilgrims arrive at Plymouth Rock

1638 CE: Galileo Galilei publishes *Two New Sciences*

1666 CE: Great London Fire

1667 CE: Milton writes *Paradise Lost*

1692 CE: Salem Witch Trials

1773 CE: Boston Tea Party

1789 CE: French Revolution

1807 CE: Fulton's first steamboat voyage

1814 CE: Brits burn Washington

1815 CE: Napoleon defeated at Battle of Waterloo

1837 CE: Victoria becomes Queen

1849 CE: California Gold Rush

1855 CE: Livingstone discovers Victoria Falls

1859 CE: Charles Darwin writes *The Origin of Species*

1861 CE: American Civil War

1865 CE: Abraham Lincoln assassinated

1869 CE: Transcontinental Railroad finished

1876 CE: Custer's Last Stand

1890 CE: Massacre at Wounded Knee

1898 CE: Spanish-American War

1903 CE: Wright Brothers make first airplane flight

1906 CE: San Francisco earthquake and fire

1908 CE: Henry Ford's Model-T rolls off the assembly line

1912 CE: Titanic sails and sinks

1914 CE: World War I

1915 CE: Einstein publishes *General Theory of Relativity*

1918 CE: Influenza kills 50 million

1927 CE: Lindbergh flies the Atlantic

1939 CE: World War II

1941 CE: Japan attacks Pearl Harbor

1944 CE: Invasion of Normandy (D-Day)

1945 CE: Nuclear warfare

1947 CE: Jackie Robinson becomes baseball's first black player

1948 CE: Mohandas Gandhi assassinated

What

SPACE PREP
0
MINUTES

PLAYER PREP
0
MINUTES

PERFORMANCE
1
MINUTES

Use These For:

Energy Expender

Group Skills

Icebreaker

Sponge

PLAYERS
1

Teach and Practice:

Blocking and Conventions

Characterization

Concentration

Creativity

Ensemble Acting

Following Directions

Group Dynamics

Listening and Silence

Memorization

Non-vocal Communication

Observation

Physical Control

Plot Structure

Spontaneity

EQUIPMENT

Bench or chair if desired.

Tell Me About the Time You ...
(TMATTY)

Directions

- One player is chosen to face the group.
- A one-minute time limit is given for the story.
- The director asks the player to "Tell me about the time you ..."
- Within the time limit, the player tells a personal story with a beginning, middle, and ending.
- The director or timekeeper signals thirty and fifteen seconds before the scene ends.

Hints for Success

- Try to catch our interest immediately. Perhaps ask a question to start with. Perhaps make a provocative statement for starters.
- Develop the plot by describing a series of conflicts leading to a crisis.
- Make sure to start the conclusion by the time you have fifteen seconds left.

Evaluation/Critique

- Did the story have a beginning, a middle, and an ending?
- Was the plot involving?
- Was the story developed fully?
- Did the conclusion make sense?
- Did the player tell the story with good energy?

Challenges and Refinements

- Play this as an icebreaker.
- To pick up the pace, have the stories be thirty to forty-five seconds.
- Use a brief headline or magazine cover as a starter.

File name on CD: TMATTY

Tell me about the time you …

accidentally blew up your neighbor's garage.

almost drowned.

ate snails.

baked a cake and forgot the sugar.

broke your arm or leg.

broke your grandmother's treasured heirloom.

crashed on a motorcycle.

dyed your hair blue.

fell into a lion's cage.

forgot your lines in a school play.

found a bottle with a genie in it.

found a hundred dollar bill.

gave the graduation speech.

got all As on your report card.

got all Fs on your report card.

got arrested for making prank phone calls.

got caught in the Bermuda Triangle.

got gum in your hair.

got lost in New York City.

got lost in the woods.

got stuck in quicksand.

had a boy/girlfriend with a tail.

had a skunk for a pet.

had an itch you couldn't scratch.

invented a new product.

lost your contact lenses.

painted your face blue.

painted your room black.

played tennis with Venus Williams.

rode a bull.

starred in a TV commercial.

threw up at a family reunion.

went around all day with your clothes on backwards.

went hiking and almost stepped on a rattlesnake.

went to Fantasy Island.

went to Paris.

were abducted by aliens.

were bitten by a St. Bernard.

were elected homecoming queen.

were in an earthquake.

were put in the hospital for a rare infectious disease.

were stepped on by an elephant.

were voted least likely to succeed.

won a beauty contest.

won a blue ribbon at the county fair.

won a spot on *The Real World.*

won a watermelon-eating contest.

won the lottery.

wrote a love letter to Tom Cruise.

SPACE PREP	PLAYER PREP	PERFORMANCE
0	**0**	**~**
MINUTES	MINUTES	MINUTES

Use These For:

Energy Expender

Group Skills

Icebreaker

Sponge

PLAYERS
Full Group

Teach and Practice:

Blocking and Conventions

Characterization

Concentration

Creativity

Ensemble Acting

Following Directions

Group Dynamics

Listening and Silence

Memorization

Non-vocal Communication

Observation

Physical Control

Plot Structure

Spontaneity

EQUIPMENT
None.

From ... To ...

Directions

- Players line up on one side of the playing area.
- The director calls out a transformation as the first player progresses from one side of the playing area to the other.
- The player makes the transformation gradually during the cross. The player may speak and create imaginary props or players as needed.
- The director may change the transformation for each player or continue with the same one to see individual variations on a theme.

Examples

- *From good to bad:* The player may start upright, smiling, handing out money to the homeless. Gradually, the smiles may change to smirks until the player is kicking/spitting at the poor homeless people.
- *From young to old:* The player starts out crawling and progresses through skipping and walking tall. Gradually the player starts to stoop and walk more slowly until at the end a walker is required for an exit.

Side Coaching

- Play your initial state!
- Make your transformation gradually!
- End the opposite of how you began!

Challenges and Refinements

This may be incorporated into *Status Slide* (page 150).

angel/devil

angry/accepting

ashamed/proud

beautiful/ugly

bored/involved

cautious/bold

certain/uncertain

confused/clear

contented/discontented

controlled/uncontrolled

coordinated/uncoordinated

cowardly/brave

criminal/victim

depressed/euphoric

Doctor Jekyll/Mr. Hyde

emotional/unemotional

excited/bored

fast/slow

fat/skinny

fearful/brave

friendly/unfriendly

frustrated/accepting

good/bad

happy/sad

hated/loved

hopeful/hopeless

intelligent/stupid

kind/nasty

lonely/involved

lost/found

man/woman

master/servant

neat/messy

nervous/calm

nervous/confident

open/closed

ordinary/extraordinary

paranoid/confident

rebellious/compliant

rejected/accepted

resentful/accepting

rich/poor

sadist/masochist

sane/insane

secure/insecure

shy/confident

sophisticated/unsophisticated

stoic/hysterical

suspicious/trusting

talented/untalented

tall/short

tense/relaxed

willing/unwilling

winner/loser

young/old

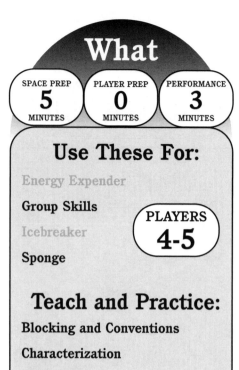

SPACE PREP
5
MINUTES

PLAYER PREP
0
MINUTES

PERFORMANCE
3
MINUTES

Use These For:

Energy Expender

Group Skills

Icebreaker

Sponge

PLAYERS
4-5

Teach and Practice:

Blocking and Conventions

Characterization

Concentration

Creativity

Ensemble Acting

Following Directions

Group Dynamics

Listening and Silence

Memorization

Non-vocal Communication

Observation

Physical Control

Plot Structure

Spontaneity

EQUIPMENT
Optional: stools, chairs, benches, and levels.

Getting There Is Half the Fun

Directions

- Divide into teams of four to five.
- Each team chooses a vehicle to feature in the improv. The team may pantomime their vehicle or make it out of chairs, stools, and levels.
- The scene starts and ends in the vehicle. All action in the scene is prompted by what might happen in the vehicle.

Example

Subway car: All players enter the subway car. Some sit; some stand. As the car begins to move, one of the passengers tries to pick another's pocket. Discovered, the would-be thief tries to escape as the doors open at the next stop.

Evaluation/Critique

- Did the players make a believable vehicle?
- Were the players able to make the vehicle appear to "move"?
- Was the vehicle used as the basis of the plot?
- Did the scene have a beginning, middle, and ending?

Vehicles

aircraft carrier

automobile

bathyscaphe

battleship

boat in the tunnel of love

Bradley vehicle

buckboard

buggy

caboose

canoe

catamaran

city bus

commercial airplane

commuter train

convertible

covered wagon

cruise ship

delivery van

dirt bike

double-decker bus

dumbwaiter

elevated train car

elevator

Ferris wheel

fighter jet

freight train

garbage truck

glider

go cart

golf cart

helicopter

hovercraft

Hummer

hydroplane

jeep

jet

jet ski

kayak

LEM (Lunar Excursion Module)

limousine

low-rider car

mine train car

monorail

motorcycle

motorcycle sidecar

narrow-gauge railway

ocean liner

parachute

passenger train

pickup truck

raft

rocket

roller coaster

rowboat

sailboat

school bus

ski lift chair

sleigh

snowmobile

soccer mom van

space shuttle

spaceship

speedboat

station wagon

stealth bomber

submarine

subway car

SUV

tank

taxi

tilt-a-whirl

tour bus

train observation car

U-2

van

water ski

yacht

Zodiac (inflatable boat)

SPACE PREP
0
MINUTES

PLAYER PREP
0
MINUTES

PERFORMANCE
~
MINUTES

Use These For:

Energy Expender

Group Skills

Icebreaker

Sponge

PLAYERS
Full Group

Teach and Practice:

Blocking and Conventions

Characterization

Concentration

Creativity

Ensemble Acting

Following Directions

Group Dynamics

Listening and Silence

Memorization

Non-vocal Communication

Observation

Physical Control

Plot Structure

Spontaneity

EQUIPMENT
None.

Walking

Directions

- The players spread out around the room.
- The director calls different walks.
- Without any talking or physical contact, the players move about the space in the different types of walks.

Side Coaching

- Concentrate on what you are doing. Forget about the other players!
- Use your entire body to accomplish your walk!
- Visualize your surroundings!

Evaluation/Critique

- Could the players feel the physical tension in their bodies?
- Could the players feel the physical differences in each different walk?
- Did the director see physical variety?

Challenges and Refinements

Play *Duck, Duck, Goose* with this difference: When the person is tagged, the director calls out a walk. Rather than racing to the empty place, the winner is chosen by the director or group for having the best walk.

Walking In/On/Through ...

a narrow log

a narrow log over a crocodile-
  infested river

a narrow path

a quickly moving sidewalk

a steep hill

a swamp

a swing bridge over a gorge

boardwalk

broken glass

broken sidewalk

cobblestone street

crocodile-infested swamp

deep snow

flooding waters

ice underneath snow

Jell-o

molasses

mud

pit of poisonous snakes

quicksand

rocky ground

slippery sidewalk

snow

spaghetti

the bottom of the ocean with
  weights on your feet

the moon

thick chocolate syrup

traffic

Walking with Different Moods

agitated

angry

anxious

athletic

awed

bouncy

breezy

buoyant

casual

cautious

chaotic

cheerful

concerned

confident

confused

cool

coordinated

debonair

dejected

determined

disoriented

distressed

dragging

elated

elegant

enthusiastic

excited

fatigued

fearful

fidgety

flexible

flirtatious

formal

frightened

grand

halfhearted

halting

hopeful

hopeless

informal

insecure

jaunty

jittery

jumpy

laconic

laid back

lazy

loose

nervous

nimble

odd

paranoid

perky

poised

ponderous

purposeful

quick

quivering

regal

relaxed

reserved

restrained

reticent

rigid

seductive

serious

shaking

shivering

shy

sloppy

sophisticated

sprightly

springy

stiff

studied

suave

supple

tense

tentative

terrified

tight

Walks

tired
trembling
troubled
twitching
unafraid
unassuming
unconstrained
uncoordinated
uneasy
uptight
vigorous
wired
withdrawn
zigzagging
zippy

Walking on the Way to ...

a dreaded blind date
a funeral
a police car after being
    arrested for shoplifting
a wedding
an awards ceremony to
    receive your award
detention
kindergarten on the first day
the principal's office
your execution

Walking in Types of Weather

balmy
blizzard
breezy
bright
brisk
chilly
clear
cloudy

crisp
dark
downpour
drizzling
drought
dry
dusty
flood
foggy
gale force winds
hail
heat wave
high clouds
humid
hurricane
lightning
low ceiling
mist
muggy
murky
overcast
partly cloudy
rain
scattered showers
showers
sleet
small craft warnings
smoggy
smoky
snow
snow showers
spitting snow
sunshine
sweltering
thunder
tidal wave
tornado
typhoon

virga
whiteout (snow)
windy

Walking as an Animal

aardvark
alligator
alpaca
ant
anteater
armadillo
badger
barracuda
bat
bear
Bigfoot
blue jay
buffalo
butterfly
camel
cat
centipede
cheetah
chicken
chimpanzee
chipmunk
clam
cow
coyote
crab
crocodile
deer
dinosaur
dog
dolphin
dragon
dragonfly
duck

eagle
eel
elephant
elephant seal
emu
ferret
fish
frog
gazelle
giraffe
goat
goldfish
goose
gopher
gorilla
hamster
hawk
hippopotamus
hog
horse
human
hummingbird
hyena
ibex
ibis
iguana
jellyfish
kangaroo
koala
lemming
lemur
leopard
lion
llama
lobster
Loch Ness Monster
lynx
manatee

manta ray
mink
monkey
moth
mouse
opossum
orangutan
orca
ostrich
otter
owl
panda
parakeet
parrot
penguin
pig
porcupine
rabbit
raccoon
rat
rattlesnake
raven
rhinoceros
roadrunner
robin
rooster
saber-toothed tiger
scallop
scorpion
sea lion
seagull
seal
shark
sheep
skunk
snail
snake
spider

squirrel
sting-ray
swan
tiger
toad
tortoise
turkey
turtle
unicorn
weasel
whale
wolf
wolverine
woodpecker
woolly mammoth
yak
yeti
zebra

SPACE PREP	PLAYER PREP	PERFORMANCE
0	**0**	**2**
MINUTES	MINUTES	MINUTES

While A ...

Use These For:

Energy Expender

Group Skills

Icebreaker

Sponge

PLAYERS
2

Teach and Practice:

Blocking and Conventions

Characterization

Concentration

Creativity

Ensemble Acting

Following Directions

Group Dynamics

Listening and Silence

Memorization

Non-vocal Communication

Observation

Physical Control

Plot Structure

Spontaneity

EQUIPMENT
None.

Directions

- Divide into teams of two.
- Each pair draws a type of weather or atmospheric condition.
- The audience suggests a *Generic Scene* (page 71), a *Film Title* (page 61), or a *Relationship* (page 151).
- The pair acts out a scene in which the type of weather focuses the action of the scene.

Example

- *Downpour:* Lovers go for a picnic that gets rained out. In the process they find an abandoned cabin, light a fire, and he proposes.
- *Heat wave:* Tourists sightseeing in London have come dressed for colder weather. As they go from place to place they gradually develop heat stroke, and one ends up in the hospital.

Side Coaching

- How do you feel in this weather?
- Show us how the weather affects your body and mood!

Evaluation/Critique

- Did the players show how the weather affected them?
- Were there many different physical reactions to the weather?
- Did the type of weather contribute to the plot?

Challenges and Refinements

- Add weather, place, and an object for a game of *In a ... With a ... While a ...* (page 118).
- Choose a scene and add the weather part way through the scene.

Weather

aurora	ground fog	Santa Ana
balmy	hail	scattered showers
blizzard	heat wave	showers
breezy	high clouds	sirocco
bright	humid	sleet
brisk	hurricane	small craft warnings
chilly	ice storm	smoggy
Chinook	icy	smoky
clear	La Niña	snow showers
cloudy	lightly falling snow	snowstorm
crisp	lightning	spitting snow
dark	low ceiling	squall
downpour	mist	sunshine
drizzling	mistral	sweltering
drought	monsoon	thunder
dry	muggy	tidal wave
dust devil	murky	tornado
dust storm	northeaster	tropical storm
dusty	overcast	typhoon
El Niño	partly cloudy	virga
flood	popcorn snow	whiteout (snow)
foggy	rain	windy
gale force winds	sand storm	zephyr

What

SPACE PREP	PLAYER PREP	PERFORMANCE
0	**0**	**2**
MINUTES	MINUTES	MINUTES

Use These For:

Energy Expender

Group Skills

Icebreaker

Sponge

**PLAYERS
2**

Teach and Practice:

Blocking and Conventions

Characterization

Concentration

Creativity

Ensemble Acting

Following Directions

Group Dynamics

Listening and Silence

Memorization

Non-vocal Communication

Observation

Physical Control

Plot Structure

Spontaneity

EQUIPMENT
Optional: stools, chairs, or benches.

Whose Line

Directions

- Divide into teams of two.
- Each player receives five to ten index cards/slips of paper with a line of dialogue on each. The players are not allowed to look at the lines in advance.
- The group suggests a *Film Title* (page 61) or *Generic Scene* (page 71).
- Players start the scene, establishing the who, where, and what.
- At random intervals each player turns over a card and incorporates the lines of dialogue into the scene.

Side Coaching

- Don't get too random!
- Keep to the situation!
- Fit the line to the situation, not the situation to the line.

Evaluation/Critique

- Were the players able to incorporate the lines into the scene so that the lines made sense and furthered the action?

Select cards appropriate to the players' ages, skills, and maturity.

"Whose Line" Lines

File name on CD: WhoseLine

Are these your shoes?
Are you afraid of snakes?
Are you an albino?
Are you my mother?
Back to the future.
Blondes have more fun.
Blue, blue, my love is blue.
Brussels sprouts are green.
Charge!
Did you really eat that?
Ding, dong, the witch is dead.
Do you ever cut your toenails?
Do you like green M&Ms?
Do you prefer Macs to PCs?
Do you speak Russian?
Do you think my hair looks good?
Don't come near me!
Don't contradict me!
Don't ever do that again!
Don't make me eat that!
Don't stop me; I'm going to jump!
Don't tickle me!
Don't touch that remote!
Don't you ever listen?
Follow the yellow brick road.
Geronimo!
Give me back my money!
Hello, angels.
Help!
Help, I need somebody!
Here comes the train.
Hindsight is 20/20.
I am not a crook.
I cannot tell a lie.
I can't get no satisfaction.
I didn't do it.
I have to sneeze.
I just got fired.
I love rocky road.
I love the color green.
I love you.
I missed my bus this morning.
I pledge allegiance to the flag.
I think I'm lost.
I think you should lose some weight.
I want a peanut butter sandwich.
I want more.
I won the lottery.
If I've told you once, I've told you a thousand times.
I'll take door number three.
I'm allergic to that.

I'm feeling kind of faint.
I'm so confused.
Is Woody Allen going to last?
It is a far, far better thing I do than
    I have ever done before.
It's for you.
I've never told you this before.
Last night I had the strangest dream.
Leave me alone.
Let's do lunch.
Let's go shopping.
Luke, I am your father.
Me Tarzan; you Jane.
My dog pooped on the carpet.
My mother loves me.
My nose is running.
Open this end.
Pepsi or Coke?
Play it again, Sam.
Please, I want more.
Read me a bedtime story.
Right on, Dude.
Shut up!
Sock it to me.
Stay back.
That is so disgusting.
That shirt makes you look fat.
That's enough.
That's nothing to laugh about.
The devil made me do it.
They were the best of times, they were the
    worst of times.
This end up.
Watch out below!
Watch out for the vicious dog.
What did you step in?
What's behind that door?
What's that crawling up your arm?
When did you graduate from high school?
Which side of the bed did you get up on?
Why did you do that?
Why don't you comb your hair?
Whoops!
Whoops, I did it again!
Would you go out with me?
You did what?
You have one blue eye and one brown eye.
You killed my sister.
You should always listen to your mother.
Your shoes smell.

Word Tennis

Use These For:

Energy Expender

Group Skills

PLAYERS
Full Group

Icebreaker

Sponge

Teach and Practice:

Blocking and Conventions

Characterization

Concentration

Creativity

Ensemble Acting

Following Directions

Group Dynamics

Listening and Silence

Memorization

Non-vocal Communication

Observation

Physical Control

Plot Structure

Spontaneity

EQUIPMENT
None.

Directions

- Two players go to the front of the group. They take turns naming items in a given category quickly and accurately.
- They play until one hesitates, uses a stalling word, or repeats a formerly given item. It is up to the director how much hesitation is allowed. The director signals when there is a foul.
- The person who misses sits down and is replaced with a new player.
- A new category is given, and the game starts again.
- Play continues until all actors have had a turn or until time is up.
- Note categories for the next game.

Examples

Director: Languages
Actor 1: Spanish
Actor 2: English
Actor 1: Italian
Actor 2: French

Side Coaching

- (To audience) Please do not call out ideas!
- Sorry, you took too long. Sit down, and we'll see how the next person does!

Challenges and Refinements

- The director makes it more difficult by giving more specific topics as students get used to the game.
- **Really Competitive Word Tennis:** Because one person is "out" and the other continues to another round, *Word Tennis* is competitive by nature. How it is directed determines *how* competitive the game is. If it's no big deal that one person is out and another takes his place, then an argument may be made that it lacks the competitive edge. The following suggestions will make the game more competitive. Add any or all of the items below to satisfy even the most blood-thirsty players.
  - ✏ Teams are chosen and cheer for their own players.
  - ✏ The director assumes the role of an "announcer" with declarations such as "The winner and still champion," "Will he make it for a fifth consecutive win?" etc.
  - ✏ The slightest hesitation calls for replacement of the player.
  - ✏ Points are awarded.
  - ✏ A buzzer or bell announces the end of a "round."

Bonuses

- Actors think of the way things are categorized.
- *Word Tennis* is an excellent group sponge.
- By manipulating the categories, directors can make the game suitable for all participants.
- Classroom teachers may use the game to reinforce lessons in other subjects.

Word Tennis Topics

File name on CD: WordTennis

adjectives to describe a monster

African countries

album/CD titles

animal noises

Asian countries

creative mascots

creative names for babies

creative names for sports teams

European countries

fantasy creatures

gemstones

girls' names

hands

health professions

hockey teams (pro)

ice cream flavors

Italian food

languages

magazines

metals

Mexican food

mountain ranges

movie stars

movie titles

musical instruments

names for a pet _____

names for new TV shows

names for newly-discovered stars
    or planets

names for rock bands

new musical instruments

new song titles

news magazines

newspapers

operas

parts of a cell

parts of the human body

plays

poetic devices

professions/jobs

reptiles

rivers of the world

Shakespeare's plays

shapes

singers

slang expressions

soft drink flavors/brands

song titles

South American countries

sports

sports stars

states in the U.S.

strange names for superheroes

stupid compliments

synonyms for bad

synonyms for good

synonyms for run

synonyms for walk

things that are blue

things that are boiled

things that are found in a barnyard

things that are found in a house

things that are found in an airplane

things that are found in bodies of water

things that are fried

things that are green

things that are made of plastic

things that are made with eggs

things that are made with milk

things that are mined

things that are orange

things that are purple

things that are rectangular

things that are red

things that are related to holidays

things that are slimy

things that are yellow

things that begin with "q"

things that bounce

things that can get you into trouble

things that can't be bought at Wal-Mart

things that come from the sky

things that come in cans

things that contain chocolate

things that contain sugar

things that contain water

things that crawl

things that end with "n"

things that fly

things that give light

things that hum or buzz

things that people drink

things that reflect light

things that roll

things that swim

things that travel on water

things that walk on two feet

titles for new rock songs

titles of children's books

titles of horror movies

trees

TV sitcoms

TV talk shows

useful household objects

vegetables

The Answers at the Back of the Book

Appendix 1: Dramatic Uses for Games

The following charts provide a quick reference for those planning to use games to fit a particular drama lesson or rehearsal aspect. For example, the director who wants to know the memorization skills of potential cast members might choose *The Name Game* or *I'm Going on a Trip* as a pre-casting exercise. The drama teacher who wants students to be aware of plot structure might choose to play *The Wacky Family, Genre House,* or *Death in a Restaurant*.

Page	Game	Energy Expender	Group Skills	Icebreaker	Sponge	Blocking and Conventions	Characterization	Concentration	Creativity	Ensemble Acting	Following Directions	Group Dynamics	Listening and Silence	Memorization	Non-vocal Communication	Observation	Physical Control	Plot Structure	Spontaneity
		|--- Uses ---|				|--------------------------------- To Teach and Practice ---------------------------------|												
114	Annoyance Game		•			•	•	•	•	•					•	•	•		•
110	As If ...				•		•	•	•		•		•		•	•	•		•
154	Bad Guy/Good Guy	•				•	•			•	•				•		•	•	•
56	Buddies	•				•	•								•	•	•	•	•
36	Conflict Game	•		•			•			•	•				•		•		•
134	CSI: Your Hometown	•				•	•	•	•	•		•			•	•			•
132	Death in a Restaurant	•		•		•	•	•	•				•	•	•			•	
122	Eureka!	•	•	•		•	•		•						•		•	•	•
40	Exit, Stage Right!				•	•	•		•		•				•	•	•		
60	Film Critics	•					•	•	•	•								•	
62	First Line, Last Line	•		•			•	•	•									•	•
50	Fractured Fairy Tales	•				•	•		•									•	
68	Freeze	•		•		•	•	•	•	•			•		•	•	•		•
160	From ... To ...				•			•		•					•	•	•		
20	Fruit Basket Upset		•	•				•	•		•	•				•	•		•
74	Genre House	•	•		•	•	•	•	•	•					•			•	•

176

Page	Game	Energy Expender	Group Skills	Icebreaker	Sponge	Blocking and Conventions	Characterization	Concentration	Creativity	Ensemble Acting	Following Directions	Group Dynamics	Listening and Silence	Memorization	Non-vocal Communication	Observation	Physical Control	Plot Structure	Spontaneity
		Uses				To Teach and Practice													
162	Getting There Is Half the Fun		•		•	•	•	•	•	•					•	•	•	•	•
10	Hitchhiker	•		•			•	•	•	•	•		•		•	•			•
100	I'm Going on a Trip		•		•				•		•		•	•					
14	If I Were a Skunk	•	•	•	•	•	•	•	•	•	•				•	•	•	•	•
118	In A … With A …		•		•	•	•	•	•	•	•	•	•		•	•	•	•	•
28	In a Manner of Speaking		•		•	•	•	•	•	•	•		•		•	•	•	•	•
70	In the Style Of		•			•	•		•	•			•		•	•	•	•	•
72	In This Genre		•			•	•		•	•									•
34	The Invention Of		•						•	•								•	
44	It Wasn't My Fault		•						•	•									•
23	The Job Interview		•		•	•		•					•		•			•	•
92	Line at a Time		•		•				•	•		•	•	•		•			•
96	Mixed Motivations		•		•			•	•	•					•	•	•	•	•
144	Musical Improv		•			•	•	•	•	•								•	•
22	Name Game		•	•	•		•	•	•		•		•	•					•
84	News Commentary			•	•		•	•	•	•	•					•		•	•
16	The Next-Door Neighbors		•							•	•		•						
98	Nursery Rhymes		•		•	•	•	•	•	•	•				•		•	•	•
102	Obsessed With			•	•	•	•	•	•	•					•	•	•	•	•
108	Opening and Closing Scenes		•		•	•	•	•	•	•	•				•	•	•	•	•
58	Party Mix	•	•	•	•		•			•			•				•		•

Page	Game	Energy Expender	Group Skills	Icebreaker	Sponge	Blocking and Conventions	Characterization	Concentration	Creativity	Ensemble Acting	Following Directions	Group Dynamics	Listening and Silence	Memorization	Non-vocal Communication	Observation	Physical Control	Plot Structure	Spontaneity
			Uses								To Teach and Practice								
128	Party Quirk Endowment		•	•	•	•	•	•	•	•	•				•	•	•	•	•
18	Pass the Object		•	•	•				•			•	•		•	•			•
112	Past/Present/Future		•				•	•	•	•	•					•	•		•
124	Props Freeze				•	•	•	•		•					•	•	•		
126	Puppet Choreography		•			•	•		•	•					•	•	•		
142	Scenes in Slang		•	•			•	•	•	•			•		•			•	•
140	Sensing			•	•			•	•		•		•		•	•	•		•
88	Sick				•	•	•	•	•	•					•	•	•		•
148	SPAR				•			•	•				•			•			•
150	Status Slide		•		•	•	•	•	•	•		•			•	•	•	•	•
146	Suspense		•					•	•	•	•	•	•					•	•
117	Tap In		•		•	•	•	•	•	•	•	•			•	•	•		•
46	Talk Show Game I		•	•			•			•	•								•
47	Talk Show Game II		•					•	•	•	•		•			•			•
158	Tell Me About the Time You ...			•	•				•	•								•	•
94	That's Life	•	•		•	•	•		•	•	•	•			•	•			•
42	This Sounds Like the Place		•					•	•	•			•	•					•
156	Time Travel		•			•	•		•	•					•	•	•	•	•
152	To the Rescue	•			•	•	•		•	•	•				•	•	•	•	•
66	Today's Your Lucky Day		•		•	•	•		•	•					•	•			•
38	Trapped		•					•	•	•							•	•	•

Page	Game	Energy Expender	Group Skills	Icebreaker	Sponge	Blocking and Conventions	Characterization	Concentration	Creativity	Ensemble Acting	Following Directions	Group Dynamics	Listening and Silence	Memorization	Non-vocal Communication	Observation	Physical Control	Plot Structure	Spontaneity
			Uses								To Teach and Practice								
90	Twisted		•	•	•	•	•		•	•					•	•	•	•	•
12	The Wacky Family		•				•		•	•								•	
164	Walking		•	•			•	•			•		•		•	•	•		•
86	Wax Museum		•			•	•		•	•					•		•		•
130	We Don't See Eye-to-Eye		•				•	•		•						•		•	
52	What If		•			•	•		•	•								•	•
104	What's My Line?	•	•							•			•						•
116	The Where Game		•	•	•	•	•	•	•		•					•			
168	While A ...				•	•	•	•	•	•					•	•	•	•	•
170	Whose Line				•	•	•	•	•	•								•	•
172	Word Tennis				•			•	•		•		•						•
32	Yearbook Game		•	•			•	•	•		•				•				
138	You've Got a Secret				•	•	•	•	•	•					•	•	•	•	•

Appendix 2: National Theatre Standards

The Consortium of National Arts Education Associations, through a grant administered by The National Association for Music Education (MENC), developed these standards. State standards and benchmarks will differ, but this is a place to start comparing and adapting standards to local curricula and lesson plans. All arts standards, including the theatre standards, can be found at:

ArtsEdge (http://www.artsedge.kennedy-center.org).

Education World also has standards on their website (http://www.educationworld.com/standards/national).

As many teachers have students perfect their best improvs into a formal presentation or script, a bullet before the standard means that an improvisation *may lead* to fulfilling that standard when script work is done.

We've added numbers and punctuation to the standards to make them easier to follow and to make the charts on the following pages easier to understand.

Standard 1 – Script Writing

Grades K-4 Content Standard 1

Script writing by planning and recording improvisations based on personal experience, heritage, imagination, literature, and history.

Achievement Standard

1. Students collaborate to select interrelated characters, environments, and situations for classroom dramatizations.

2. Students improvise dialogue to tell stories and formalize improvisations by writing or recording the dialogue.

Grades 5-8 Content Standard 1

Script writing by the creation of improvisations and scripted scenes based on personal experience, heritage, imagination, literature, and history.

Achievement Standard

1. Students, individually and in groups, create characters, environments, and actions that create tension and suspense.

•2. Students refine and record dialogue and action.

Grades 9-12 Content Standard 1

Script writing through improvising, writing, and refining scripts based on personal experience, heritage, imagination, literature, and history.

Achievement Standard - Proficient:

•1P. Students construct imaginative scripts and collaborate with actors to refine scripts so that story and meaning are conveyed to an audience.

Achievement Standard - Advanced:

•1A. Students write theatre, film, television, or electronic media scripts in a variety of traditional and new forms that include original characters with unique dialogue that motivates action.

Standard 2 – Acting

Grades K-4 Content Standard 2

Acting by assuming roles and interacting in improvisations.

Achievement Standard

•1. Students imagine and clearly describe characters, their relationships, and their environments.

2. Students use variations of locomotor and nonlocomotor movement and vocal pitch, tempo, and tone for different characters.

3. Students assume roles that exhibit concentration and contribute to the action of classroom dramatizations based on personal experience, heritage, imagination, literature, and history.

Grades 5-8 Content Standard 2

Acting by developing basic acting skills to portray characters who interact in improvised and scripted scenes.

Achievement Standard

1. Students analyze descriptions, dialogue, and actions to discover, articulate, and justify character motivation and invent character behaviors based on the observation of interactions, ethical choices, and emotional responses of people.

2. Students demonstrate acting skills (such as sensory recall, concentration, breath control, diction, body alignment, control of isolated body parts) to develop characterizations that suggest artistic choice.

3. Students in an ensemble interact as the invented characters.

Grades 9-12 Content Standard 2

Acting by developing, communicating, and sustaining characters in improvisations and informal or formal productions.

Achievement Standard - Proficient:

1P. Students analyze the physical, emotional, and social dimensions of characters found in dramatic texts from various genres and media.

2P. Students compare and demonstrate various classical and contemporary acting techniques and methods.

3P. Students in an ensemble create and sustain characters that communicate with audiences.

Achievement Standard - Advanced:

1A. Students demonstrate artistic discipline to achieve an ensemble in rehearsal and performance.

•2A. Students create consistent characters from classical, contemporary, realistic, and nonrealistic dramatic texts in informal and formal theatre, film, television, or electronic media productions.

Standard 3 – Designing

Grades K-4 Content Standard 3

Designing by visualizing and arranging environments for classroom dramatizations.

Achievement Standard

1. Students visualize environments and construct designs to communicate locale and mood using visual elements (such as space, color, line, shape, texture) and aural aspects using a variety of sound sources.

2. Students collaborate to establish playing spaces for classroom dramatizations and to select and safely organize available materials that suggest scenery, properties, lighting, sound, costumes, and makeup.

Grades 5-8 Content Standard 3

Designing by developing environments for improvised and scripted scenes.

Achievement Standard

•1. Students explain the functions and interrelated nature of scenery, properties, lighting, sound, costumes, and makeup in creating an environment appropriate for the drama.

•2. Students analyze improvised and scripted scenes for technical requirements.

•3. Students develop focused ideas for the environment using visual elements (line, texture, color, space), visual principles (repetition, balance, emphasis, contrast, unity), and aural qualities (pitch, rhythm, dynamics, tempo, expression) from traditional and nontraditional sources.

4. Students work collaboratively and safely to select and create elements of scenery, properties, lighting, and sound to signify environments, and costumes and makeup to suggest character.

Grades 9-12 Content Standard 3

Designing and producing by conceptualizing and realizing artistic interpretations for informal or formal productions.

Achievement Standard - Proficient:

1P. Students explain the basic physical and chemical properties of the technical aspects of theatre (such as light, color, electricity, paint, and makeup).

2P. Students analyze a variety of dramatic texts from cultural and historical perspectives to determine production requirements.

•3P. Students develop designs that use visual and aural elements to convey environments that clearly support the text.

•4P. Students apply technical knowledge and skills to collaboratively and safely create functional scenery, properties, lighting, sound, costumes, and makeup.

5P. Students design coherent stage management, promotional, and business plans.

Achievement Standard - Advanced:

1A. Students explain how scientific and technological advances have impacted set, light, sound, and costume design and implementation for theatre, film, television, or electronic media productions.

2A. Students collaborate with directors to develop unified production concepts that convey the metaphorical nature of the drama for informal and formal theatre, film, television, or electronic media productions.

3A. Students safely construct and efficiently operate technical aspects of theatre, film, television, or electronic media productions.

•4A. Students create and reliably implement production schedules, stage management plans, promotional ideas, and business and front of house procedures for informal and formal theatre, film, television, or electronic media productions.

Standard 4 – Directing

Grades K-4 Content Standard 4

Directing by planning classroom dramatizations.

Achievement Standard

1. Students collaboratively plan and prepare improvisations and demonstrate various ways of staging classroom dramatizations.

Grades 5-8 Content Standard 4

Directing by organizing rehearsals for improvised and scripted scenes.

Achievement Standard

1. Students lead small groups in planning visual and aural elements and in rehearsing improvised and scripted scenes, demonstrating social, group, and consensus skills.

Grades 9-12 Content Standard 4

Directing by interpreting dramatic texts and organizing and conducting rehearsals for informal or formal productions.

Achievement Standard - Proficient:

1P. Students develop multiple interpretations and visual and aural production choices for scripts and production ideas and choose those that are most interesting.

2P. Students justify selections of text, interpretation, and visual and aural artistic choices.

3P. Students effectively communicate directorial choices to a small ensemble for improvised or scripted scenes.

Achievement Standard - Advanced:

1A. Students explain and compare the roles and interrelated responsibilities of the various personnel involved in theatre, film, television, and electronic media productions.

•2A. Students collaborate with designers and actors to develop aesthetically unified production concepts for informal and formal theatre, film, television, or electronic media productions.

3A. Students conduct auditions, cast actors, direct scenes, and conduct production meetings to achieve production goals.

Standard 5 – Researching

(Researching, rarely used with improvisation, is not included in the chart.)

Grades K-4 Content Standard 5

Researching by finding information to support classroom dramatizations.

Achievement Standard

1. Students communicate information to peers about people, events, time, and place related to classroom dramatizations.

Grades 5-8 Content Standard 5

Researching by using cultural and historical information to support improvised and scripted scenes.

Achievement Standard

1. Students apply research from print and non-print sources to script writing, acting, design, and directing choices.

Grades 9-12 Content Standard 5

Researching by evaluating and synthesizing cultural and historical information to support artistic choices.

Achievement Standard - Proficient:

1P. Students identify and research cultural, historical, and symbolic clues in dramatic texts and evaluate the validity and practicality of the information to assist in making artistic choices for informal and formal productions.

Achievement Standard - Advanced:

1A. Students research and describe appropriate historical production designs, techniques, and performances from various cultures to assist in making artistic choices for informal and formal theatre, film, television, or electronic media productions.

Standard 6 – Comparing Art Forms

(Comparing Art Forms, rarely used with improvisation, is not included in the chart.)

Grades K-4 Content Standard 6

Comparing and connecting art forms by describing theatre, dramatic media (such as film, television, and electronic media), and other art forms.

Achievement Standard

1. Students describe visual, aural, oral, and kinetic elements in theatre, dramatic media, dance, music, and visual arts.

2. Students compare how ideas and emotions are expressed in theatre, dramatic media, dance, music, and visual arts.

3. Students select movement, music, or visual elements to enhance the mood of a classroom dramatization.

Grades 5-8 Content Standard 6

Comparing and incorporating art forms by analyzing methods of presentation and audience response for theatre, dramatic media (such as film, television, and electronic media), and other art forms.

Achievement Standard

1. Students describe characteristics and compare the presentation of characters, environments, and actions in theatre, musical theatre, dramatic media, dance, and visual arts.

2. Students incorporate elements of dance, music, and visual arts to express ideas and emotions in improvised and scripted scenes.

3. Students express and compare personal reactions to several art forms.

4. Students describe and compare the functions and interaction of performing and visual artists and audience members in theatre, dramatic media, musical theatre, dance, music, and visual arts.

Grades 9-12 Content Standard 6

Comparing and integrating art forms by analyzing traditional theatre, dance, music, visual arts, and new art forms.

Achievement Standard - Proficient:

1P. Students describe and compare the basic nature, materials, elements, and means of communicating in theatre, dramatic media, musical theatre, dance, music, and the visual arts.

2P. Students determine how the non-dramatic art forms are modified to enhance the expression of ideas and emotions in theatre.

3P. Students illustrate the integration of several arts media in informal presentations.

Achievement Standard - Advanced:

1A. Students compare the interpretive and expressive natures of several art forms in a specific culture or historical period.

2A. Students compare the unique interpretive and expressive natures and aesthetic qualities of traditional arts from various cultures and historical periods with contemporary new art forms (such as performance art).

3A. Students integrate several arts and/or media in theatre, film, television, or electronic media productions.

Standard 7 – Analyzing

Grades K-4 Content Standard 7

Analyzing and explaining personal preferences and constructing meanings from classroom dramatizations and from theatre, film, television, and electronic media productions.

Achievement Standard

1. Students identify and describe the visual, aural, oral, and kinetic elements of classroom dramatizations and dramatic performances.

2. Students explain how the wants and needs of characters are similar to and different from their own.

3. Students articulate emotional responses to and explain personal preferences about the whole as well as the parts of dramatic performances.

4. Students analyze classroom dramatizations and students' contributions to the collaborative process of developing improvised and scripted scenes.

Grades 5-8 Content Standard 7

Analyzing, evaluating, and constructing meanings from improvised and scripted scenes and from theatre, film, television, and electronic media productions.

Achievement Standard

1. Students describe and analyze the effect of publicity, study guides, programs, and physical environments on audience response and appreciation of dramatic performances.

2. Students articulate and support the meanings constructed from their and others' dramatic performances.

3. Students use articulated criteria to describe, analyze, and constructively evaluate the perceived effectiveness of artistic choices found in dramatic performances.

4. Students describe and evaluate the perceived effectiveness of students' contributions to the collaborative process of developing improvised and scripted scenes.

Grades 9-12 Content Standard 7

Analyzing, critiquing, and constructing meanings from informal and formal theatre, film, television, and electronic media productions.

Achievement Standard - Proficient:

1P. Students construct social meanings from informal and formal productions and from dramatic performances from a variety of cultures and historical periods and relate these to current personal, national, and international issues.

•2P. Students articulate and justify personal aesthetic criteria for critiquing dramatic texts and events that compare perceived artistic intent with the final aesthetic achievement.

•3P. Students analyze and critique the whole and the parts of dramatic performances, taking into account the context and constructively suggest alternative artistic choices.

4P. Students constructively evaluate their own and others' collaborative efforts and artistic choices in informal and formal productions.

Achievement Standard - Advanced:

1A. Students construct personal meanings from nontraditional dramatic performances.

•2A. Students analyze, compare, and evaluate differing critiques of the same dramatic texts and performances.

3A. Students critique several dramatic works in terms of other aesthetic philosophies (such as the underlying ethos of Greek drama, French classicism with its unities of time and place, Shakespeare and romantic forms, India classical drama, Japanese kabuki, and others).

•4A. Students analyze and evaluate critical comments about personal dramatic work explaining which points are most appropriate to inform further development of the work.

Standard 8 – Understanding

(Understanding, as used in these Standards, is not part of improv and is not included in the chart.)

Grades K-4 Content Standard 8

Understanding context by recognizing the role of theatre, film, television, and electronic media in daily life.

Achievement Standard

1. Students identify and compare similar characters and situations in stories and dramas from and about various cultures, illustrate with classroom dramatizations, and discuss how theatre reflects life.

2. Students identify and compare the various settings and reasons for creating dramas and attending theatre, film, television, and electronic media productions.

Grades 5-8 Content Standard 8

Understanding context by analyzing the role of theatre, film, television, and electronic media in the community and in other cultures.

Achievement Standard

1. Students describe and compare universal characters and situations in dramas from and about various cultures and historical periods, illustrate in improvised and scripted scenes, and discuss how theatre reflects a culture.

2. Students explain the knowledge, skills, and discipline needed to pursue careers and vocational opportunities in theatre, film, television, and electronic media.

3. Students analyze the emotional and social impact of dramatic events in their lives, in the community, and in other cultures.

4. Students explain how culture affects the content and production values of dramatic performances.

5. Students explain how social concepts such as cooperation, communication, collaboration, consensus, self-esteem, risk taking, sympathy, and empathy apply in theatre and daily life.

Grades 9-12 Content Standard 8

Understanding context by analyzing the role of theatre, film, television, and electronic media in the past and the present.

Achievement Standard - Proficient:

1P. Students compare how similar themes are treated in drama from various cultures and historical periods, illustrate with informal performances, and discuss how theatre can reveal universal concepts.

2P. Students identify and compare the lives, works, and influence of representative theatre artists in various cultures and historical periods.

3P. Students identify cultural and historical sources of American theatre and musical theatre.

4P. Students analyze the effect of their own cultural experiences on their dramatic work.

Achievement Standard - Advanced:

1A. Students analyze the social and aesthetic impact of underrepresented theatre and film artists.

2A. Students analyze the relationships among cultural values, freedom of artistic expression, ethics, and artistic choices in various cultures and historical periods.

3A. Students analyze the development of dramatic forms, production practices, and theatrical traditions across cultures and historical periods and explain influences on contemporary theatre, film, television, and electronic media productions.

Applying National Theatre Standards to Improv Games

The next 6 pages will help you align the games in *Improv Ideas* to your state's standards. We hope you'll be pleased with how well many games fulfill the educational theatrical standards.

Page Game	1. Script Writing						2. Acting								
	K-4 1	K-4 2	5-8 1	5-8 2 *	9-12 1P *	9-12 1A *	K-4 1 *	K-4 2	K-4 3	5-8 1	5-8 2	5-8 3	9-12 2P	9-12 3P	9-12 1A
114 Annoyance Game	•	•	•			•	•	•	•	•	•		•	•	•
110 As If …			•				•			•	•				
154 Bad Guy/Good Guy	•	•				•	•	•	•	•	•	•	•		•
56 Buddies	•	•	•				•	•	•	•	•		•		•
36 Conflict Game	•	•	•	•	•	•	•	•	•	•	•	•	•		•
134 CSI: Your Hometown	?	?	•	•	•	•	?	?	?	•	•	•	•		•
132 Death in a Restaurant	?	?	•			•	?	?	?	•	•	•	•		•
122 Eureka!	•	•	•	•	•	•	•	•	•	•	•	•	•		•
40 Exit, Stage Right!						•		•	•	•			•		
60 Film Critics	•	•	•	•	•	•	•	•	•	•	•	•	•		•
62 First Line, Last Line	•	•	•	•	•	•	•	•	•	•	•	•		•	•
50 Fractured Fairy Tales	•	•	•			•	•	•	•	•	•			•	•
68 Freeze	•	•	•	•	•	•	•	•	•	•	•	•	•	•	•
160 From … To …			•	•		•	•	•		•	•			•	
20 Fruit Basket Upset															
74 Genre House	•	•	•				•	•	•	•	•	•	•		•
162 Getting There Is Half the Fun	•	•	•	•	•	•	•	•	•	•	•		•	•	•
10 Hitchhiker	•	•				•	•	•	•	•	•		•		•
100 I'm Going on a Trip											•				•
14 If I Were a Skunk	Applications depend on which game is chosen to act as animals.														
118 In A … With A …	•	•	•				•	•	•	•	•	•		•	•

186

Key to the Symbols and Numbers

K-4, 5-8, 9-12 = the grade level of the standard
1, 2, 3P, 4A, etc. = the achievement standard number from pages 180-185
* = standard may be fulfilled when an improv is made into a formal script
• = fulfills or leads to fulfillment of standard
? = please evaluate the maturity and skills of younger players before trying this game

K-4 1	K-4 2	5-8 1*	5-8 2*	5-8 3*	9-12 3P*	9-12 4P*	9-12 4A*	K-4 1	5-8 1	9-12 1P	9-12 2P	9-12 3P	9-12 2A*	K-4 1	K-4 2	K-4 3	K-4 4	5-8 2	5-8 3*	5-8 4*	9-12 2P*	9-12 3P*	9-12 4P*	9-12 2A*	9-12 4A*
3. Designing								**4. Directing**						**7. Analyzing**											
•	•							•	•	•	•	•	•	•	•	•	•	•	•	•	•	•	•	•	•
•			•					•			•	•		•	•						•		•		•
?	?							?	?					?	?	?	?				•		•		•
	•			•				•	•	•	•		•	•	•	•	•	•	•	•	•	•	•	•	•
	•							•	•	•	•	•	•	•	•	•	•	•	•	•	•	•	•	•	•
?	?		•					?	?	•	•	•	•	?	?	?	?	•	•	•	•	•	•	•	•
•	•													•	•	•	•	•	•	•		•	•		•
•	•	•	•			•		•						•	•	•	•	•	•	•	•	•	•	•	
•	•	•		•		•		•	•	•	•		•	•	•	•	•	•	•	•	•	•	•	•	•
•	•		•		•		•	•			•	•		•	•	•	•	•	•	•	•	•	•	•	•
•	•		•	•				•	•	•	•	•	•	•	•	•	•	•	•	•	•	•	•	•	•
•	•		•	•				•	•	•	•	•	•	•	•	•	•	•	•	•	•	•	•	•	•
•	•	•	•	•	•	•	•	•	•	•				•	•	•	•	•	•	•	•	•	•	•	•
•														•	•	•	•	•	•	•	•	•	•	•	•
•	•																								

Applications depend on which game is chosen to act as animals.

| • | • | | | | | | | • | • | • | | • | | • | • | • | • | • | • | • | • | • | • | • | • |

Page — Game	1. Script Writing						2. Acting								
	K-4 1	K-4 2	5-8 1	5-8 2 *	9-12 1P *	9-12 1A *	K-4 1 *	K-4 2	K-4 3	5-8 1	5-8 2	5-8 3	9-12 2P	9-12 3P	9-12 1A
28 In a Manner of Speaking	?	?	•		•	•	?	?	?	•	•	•			•
70 In the Style Of	•	•	•			•	•	•	•	•	•	•	•	•	•
72 In This Genre	•	•	•	•		•	•	•	•	•	•	•	•	•	•
34 The Invention Of	•	•	•	•	•	•	•	•	•	•	•	•		•	•
44 It Wasn't My Fault															
23 The Job Interview	•	•	•	•	•	•	•	•	•	•	•	•	•	•	•
92 Line at a Time											•				•
96 Mixed Motivations	•	•	•	•	•	•	•	•	•	•	•	•	•	•	•
144 Musical Improv	?	?	•	•	•	•	?	?	?	•	•	•	•	•	•
22 Name Game							•								
84 News Commentary	•	•	•	•	•	•	•	•	•	•	•	•	•	•	•
16 The Next-Door Neighbors	•	•	•	•	•	•	•	•	•	•	•	•		•	•
98 Nursery Rhymes	•	•	•	•	•	•	•	•	•	•	•	•		•	•
102 Obsessed With	•	•	•					•	•	•	•	•	•	•	•
108 Opening and Closing Scenes	•	•	•	•	•	•	•	•	•	•	•			•	•
58 Party Mix	?	?					?	?							
128 Party Quirk Endowments	?	?					?	?	?			•		•	•
18 Pass the Object								•		•					
112 Past/Present/Future	?	?	•	•	•	•	?	?	?	•	•	•		•	•
124 Props Freeze	•						•	•	•						
126 Puppet Choreography	•		•		•	•	•	•	•	•	•	•	•	•	•
142 Scenes in Slang	?	?	•			•	?	?	?	•	•	•		•	•
140 Sensing												•			
88 Sick	?	?	?	?	•	•	?	?	?	?	?	?	•	•	•
148 SPAR	?	?					?	?	?						

K-4 1	K-4 2	5-8 1*	5-8 2*	5-8 3*	9-12 3P*	9-12 4P*	9-12 4A*	K-4 1	5-8 1	9-12 1P	9-12 2P	9-12 3P	9-12 2A*	K-4 1	K-4 2	K-4 3	K-4 4	5-8 2	5-8 3*	5-8 4*	9-12 2P*	9-12 3P*	9-12 4P*	9-12 2A*	9-12 4A*
3. Designing								**4. Directing**						**7. Analyzing**											
?	?							?	•	•		•		?	?	?	?		•	•	•	•		•	•
•	•		•	•	•	•		•	•	•	•	•		•	•	•	•	•	•	•	•	•	•	•	•
•	•	•	•	•	•	•		•	•	•		•		•	•	•	•		•	•	•	•	•	•	•
•	•							•	•	•		•		•		•	•	•	•	•	•	•	•	•	•
•	•				•	•								•	•										
•	•								•				•	•	•	•	•	•	•	•	•	•	•	•	•
•		•										•		•											
•	•	•	•		•	•	•	•					•	•	•	•	•	•	•	•	•	•	•	•	•
•	•	•	•		•	•	•	•	•	•	•	•	•	•	•	•	•	•	•	•	•	•	•	•	•
•	•	•		•		•		•	•	•	•	•		•	•	•	•	•	•	•	•	•	•	•	•
•	•		•					•	•	•	•	•	•	•	•			•					•		•
•	•							•	•	•	•	•	•	•	•	•	•	•	•	•	•	•	•	•	•
•	•					•		•	•			•		•	•	•		•	•	•	•	•	•	•	•
																			•	•	•	•	•	•	•
?	?	•	•					?	?	•	•	•	•	?	?	?	?	•	•	•	•	•	•	•	•
•	•	•	•	•	•	•	•	•	•	•	•	•	•	•	•	•	•	•	•	•	•	•	•	•	•
?	?							?	?	•	•		•	?	?	?	?	•	•	•	•	•	•	•	•
?	?	•	•	•	•	•	•	?	?	•	•	•	•	?	?	?	?	•	•	•	•	•	•	•	•
?	?							?	?		•		•	?	?	?	?	?	?	?	•	•	•	•	•
?	?		•	•			•	?	?		•		•	?	?	?	?	•	•	•	•	•	•	•	•

Page	Game	K-4 1	K-4 2	5-8 1	5-8 2 *	9-12 1P *	9-12 1A *	K-4 1 *	K-4 2	K-4 3	5-8 1	5-8 2	5-8 3	9-12 2P	9-12 3P	9-12 1A
		1. Script Writing						**2. Acting**								
150	Status Slide	?	?	•			•	?	?	?	•	•	•		•	•
146	Suspense	•	•	•	•	•	•	•	•	•	•	•	•	•	•	•
117	Tap In	•	•	•				•	•	•	•	•	•	•		
46	Talk Show Game I	•	•	•			•	•	•	•	•	•			•	•
47	Talk Show Game II	?	?					?	?	•	•		•		•	
158	Tell Me About the Time You ...	•	•	•			•	•			•	•			•	
94	That's Life	•	•	•	•	•	•	•	•	•	•	•	•	•	•	•
42	This Sounds Like the Place			•		•										
156	Time Travel	•	•	•	•	•	•	•	•	•	•	•	•	•	•	•
152	To the Rescue	•	•	•	•	•	•	•	•	•	•	•	•		•	•
66	Today's Your Lucky Day	•	•	•	•	•		•	•	•	•	•	•	•	•	•
38	Trapped	•	•	•	•	•	•	•	•	•	•	•	•	•	•	•
90	Twisted	?	?	?	?			?	?	?	?	?	?			
12	The Wacky Family	•	•	•	•	•	•	•	•	•	•	•	•	•	•	•
164	Walking							•		•	•	•			•	
86	Wax Museum	•		•			•	•	•	•	•	•	•		•	•
130	We Don't See Eye-to-Eye	•	•	•			•	•	•	•	•	•	•		•	•
52	What If	•	•	•	•	•	•	•	•	•	•	•	•		•	•
104	What's My Line?	?	?					?	?	?				•		
116	The Where Game	•	•	•	•	•	•	•	•	•	•	•	•		•	•
168	While A ...	•	•	•		•	•	•	•	•	•	•	•	•	•	•
170	Whose Line	?	?	•			•					•	•		•	•
172	Word Tennis								•						•	
32	Yearbook Game	•						•		•	•	•			•	
138	You've Got a Secret	?	?	•		•	•	?	?	?			•		•	•

3. Designing

K-4 1	K-4 2	5-8 1 *	5-8 2 *	5-8 3 *	9-12 3P *	9-12 4P *	9-12 4A *
?	?			•			•
?	?						
•	•						
•	•	•	•				
?	?	•	•	•			
•	•						•
•	•	•	•	•	•	•	
•	•			•	•	•	•
		•	•	•	•	•	•
•	•				•		•
•	•	•		•	•	•	
?	?	?	?	?			
•		•		•			
•	•	•	•	•	•	•	•
•	•	•	•	•	•		
•	•	•	•	•			•
?	?	?	?	?			
•	•			•			•
•	•	•			•		•
•				•			
?	?		•		•		•
•	•			•	•	•	
?	?		•				•

4. Directing

K-4 1	5-8 1	9-12 1P	9-12 2P	9-12 3P	9-12 2A *
?	?				•
?	?		•		•
		•	•		•
?	•	•	•	•	•
•	•	•			•
•	•				•
			•		•
					•
•	•	•	•	•	•
?	?				
•			•		
•	•	•	•	•	•
•	•	•	•	•	•
•	•	•	•	•	
?					
•	•	•	•	•	•
•	•				
?	?	•	•	•	•
•	•	•			•
?	?	•		•	•

7. Analyzing

K-4 1	K-4 2	K-4 3	K-4 4	5-8 2	5-8 3 *	5-8 4 *	9-12 2P *	9-12 3P *	9-12 4P *	9-12 2A *	9-12 4A *
?	?	?	?	•	•		•			•	•
?	?	?	?	•	•	•	•	•	•	•	•
•	•	•	•	•	•	•		•			
•	•	•	•	•	•	•	•	•	•	•	•
?	?	?	?	•	•	•	•	•	•	•	•
•	•	•	•	•	•	•	•	•	•	•	•
•	•	•	•	•	•	•	•	•	•	•	•
•	•		•			•					
•	•	•	•	•	•	•	•	•	•	•	•
•	•	•	•	•		•	•		•		•
•	•	•	•	•	•	•	•	•	•	•	•
•	•	•	•	•	•	•	•	•	•	•	•
?	?	?	?	?	?	?	•		•	•	•
•	•	•	•	•	•	•	•	•	•	•	•
•	•	•	•	•	•	•	•	•	•	•	•
•	•	•	•	•	•	•	•	•	•	•	•
•	•	•	•	•	•	•	•	•	•	•	•
•	•	•	•	•	•	•	•	•	•	•	•
?	?	?	?		•		•			•	•
•	•	•	•	•		•		•		•	•
•	•	•	•	•	•	•	•	•	•	•	•
•	•	•	•	•	•	•	•	•			
?	?	?	?	•	•	•	•	•	•	•	•
•	•	•	•	•	•	•	•	•	•	•	•
?	?	?	?	•	•		•		•	•	•

Appendix 3: Gimmicks and Other Useful Tools

You've Gotta Have a Gimmick!

Why gimmicks?

People love gimmicks, especially younger students. When we first started teaching improv, we used the time-honored technique of asking the group for ideas. After dealing with the off-the-wall answers and — sometimes — even silence, we started using the ideas lists. We put slips of paper in a large cup and let them draw. When the slips weren't returned, we put them on index cards in a big black hat. Then a fishbowl. We quickly realized that the cards needed to be sturdier, so we enlisted the use of a laminator and put the ideas on sturdy tag board. Picking a card out of a hat seemed to be as much fun as the improv itself.

Spinergy

But variety is the spice of life, so we started using other aids as well. Luckily, a local board game designer came by Justine's classroom to test her game. *Spinergy* consists of a sturdy plastic wheel that can hold three transparent rings of words. When players spin the three rings they arrive with a combination of words such as "plastic," "pup tent," and "fearful." The object of the game is to use a scenario card: "You are breaking up with your significant other. Make up an excuse and act out the scenario incorporating the three words." These mix-and-match ideas could be used on cards as well. For example, *In A … With A …* could be played using words from each of the lists, *Places*, *Objects*, and *Weather*. Obviously the uniqueness of the "gimmick" is entrancing to the students.

Card decks

There are many other gimmicks available. Tarot cards are often very colorful and can be used to inspire scenes. We use nontraditional decks such as the Osho Zen Tarot or the Celtic Wisdom Deck, as these are unusually intriguing and consist of cards with one word concepts such as "success" and "sorrow." There is no need to identify them as tarot decks, and they might be considered inappropriate in some settings. Other card games can be quite useful as well.

Visual imagery

Similarly, using prints of photographs or paintings can elicit ideas for improvs (save those calendars!). Paint words on small flat stones then seal or varnish them. We've even laminated bumper stickers and tabloid headlines. If you have access to a button maker, make buttons with character traits and emotions.

Movie plot generator

Justine discovered a fascinating gimmick in a drama bookstore in New York. *The Official Movie Plot Generator* is both a book and a gimmick. It consists of ninety flip-cards that can be arranged in any order — "27,000 hilarious movie plot combinations" according to its authors, the Brothers Heimberg. Sample "plots" include: "A single man | travels through time | to win the heart of the high school dream boat" or "A hockey-mask wearing psychopath | gets transformed into a gorgeous sex pot | in the middle of downtown Tokyo (in Japanese with English subtitles)." The ideas are out there, and players love to make up their own. It's just a matter of using them and incorporating them into your work.

Multimedia ideas

Another successful "gimmick" is the use of noisemakers as timers. Participants love gongs, buzzers, whistles, bells, and hand clappers. Be creative! The younger the participants, the more they appreciate the variety (and creativity) that goes into making the improvs truly multimedia.

A cautionary tale

This brings us to another "gimmick" that is more controversial: video. We are required to videotape many of our sessions, but find that this often interferes with the spontaneity. We would recommend that this be used sparingly, as it can seem an unnecessary intrusion and can often interfere with the process aspect of the work. Unless you are using improv solely as a means of preparing a production, it is often better to simply put the cameras away. So, even though we are in the wonderful world of technology, often more technology leads to less creativity. We recommend a return to simplicity with our "gimmicks." Rain sticks. Cookie sheets. Less, quite often, is more!

Persuasion and Propaganda Techniques

- Use supporting evidence such as facts, examples, and expert opinions.
- Distort the facts.
- Use flattery.
- Use the bandwagon approach of "everybody is doing it."
- Use an excess of science.
- Quote statistics and use them to mean what *you* want them to mean.
- Use loaded phrases like "of course," "obviously," and "as you know."
- Make an emotional appeal.
- Use big words to imply that you are knowledgeable.
- Say that a famous person or celebrity agrees with your point of view.
- Use the "just plain folks" technique to identify your opinion with wholesome values.
- Bring out negative feelings by name-calling.
- Use glittering generalities that are so general that they cannot be disproved.
- Tell people what they want to hear.
- Link statements that do not necessarily follow.
- Point out your opponent's weaknesses or the weaknesses of his argument.
- Stack the deck. Tell all that's good about your argument and all that's bad about your opponent's.
- Use and distort logic.

Stage Area Map

Up Right	Up Center	Up Left
Center Right	Center	Center Left
Down Right	Down Center	Down Left

Audience

FYI

What you need to play.
(You will *always* need a list.)

Key to the Symbols and Numbers
Y = Yes
N = No
F = Full Group
O = Optional
~ = Open ended

	Players	Equipment	Space Prep	Player Prep	Performance
				Time Per Group	
114 Annoyance Game	2	Y	2	3	3
110 As If ...	F	N	0	0	5
154 Bad Guy/Good Guy	2	Y	2	0	2-3
56 Buddies	2	N	0	0	2
36 Conflict Game	2	N	0	3	3-5
134 CSI: Your Hometown	4-6	Y	1	10	5
132 Death in a Restaurant	6	Y	2	2	10
122 Eureka!	4	N	0	5	1-3
40 Exit, Stage Right!	F	Y	0	0	1
60 Film Critics	5	Y	0	0	<10
62 First Line, Last Line	2	N	0	0	1
50 Fractured Fairy Tales	4-5	Y	3	5	5
68 Freeze	5-6	Y	2	0	3
160 From ... To ...	F	N	0	0	~
20 Fruit Basket Upset	F	Y	2	0	~
74 Genre House	3-5	Y	2	0	5
162 Getting There Is Half the Fun	4-5	O	5	0	3
10 Hitchhiker	5	Y	2	0	~
100 I'm Going on a Trip	F	N	0	0	~
14 If I Were a Skunk	3-5	Y	0	3	3
118 In A ... With A ...	2	N	0	0	1-3
28 In a Manner of Speaking	2	N	2	0	2
70 In the Style Of	2-4	Y	2	0	5
72 In This Genre	3-5	Y	2	5	3
34 The Invention Of	4-5	Y	0	3	3-5
44 It Wasn't My Fault	F	N	0	0	<15
23 The Job Interview	2	Y	2	0	3
92 Line at a Time	F	N	0	0	~
96 Mixed Motivations	2	N	0	0	3
144 Musical Improv	2	N	0	0	~
22 Name Game	F	Y	2	0	~
84 News Commentary	2	Y	2	0	3
16 The Next-Door Neighbors	4-5	Y	2	0	~
98 Nursery Rhymes	2-4	N	0	3	5
102 Obsessed With	2	Y	1	3	2-3
108 Opening and Closing Scenes	2	N	0	0	2-3
58 Party Mix	F	Y	~	~	~
128 Party Quirk Endowments	4-5	N	0	3	<5
18 Pass the Object	F	Y	1	0	~
112 Past/Present/Future	4	Y	3	3	3-5
124 Props Freeze	5	Y	0	3	<1
126 Puppet Choreography	5	Y	3	30	3
142 Scenes in Slang	2	N	0	1	2
140 Sensing	F	N	0	2	~
88 Sick	2	O	0	0	~
148 SPAR	2	N	0	0	6
150 Status Slide	2	N	0	5	3
146 Suspense	5	Y	5	5	3
117 Tap In	F	N	0	0	~
46 Talk Show Game I	3-5	Y	3	0	~
47 Talk Show Game II	3-5	Y	5	0	~
158 Tell Me About the Time You ...	1	O	0	0	1
94 That's Life	3-4	N	0-2	0	~
42 This Sounds Like the Place	F	Y	2	0	~
156 Time Travel	2-4	Y	2	0	5
152 To the Rescue	2	N	0	0	2-3
66 Today's Your Lucky Day	2-4	Y	5	0	5
38 Trapped	3-5	N	0	5	1
90 Twisted	3-7	Y	2	0	5
12 The Wacky Family	5	N	0	3	3
164 Walking	F	N	0	0	~
86 Wax Museum	4-6	O	2	5	2
130 We Don't See Eye-to-Eye	2	N	0	0	1-3
52 What If	4-5	Y	5	10	~
104 What's My Line?	4	Y	2	0	<5
116 The Where Game	F	N	0	0	<5
168 While A ...	2	N	0	0	2
170 Whose Line	2	O	0	0	2
172 Word Tennis	F	N	0	0	~
32 Yearbook Game	5-7	Y	5	1	1
138 You've Got a Secret	2	N	0	0	2

Resources

www.improvideas.com

Belt, Lynda. *Improv Game Book Two.* Thespis Productions, 1993.

Belt, Lynda and Rebecca Stockley. *Acting Through Improv/Improv Through Theatre Sports.* Thespis Productions, 1995.

Benedetti, Robert. *The Actor at Work.* Allyn & Bacon, Inc., 2004.

Bernardi, Philip. *Improvisation Starters.* F&W Publications, Inc., 1992.

Blatner, Adam and Allee Blatner. *The Art of Play.* Revised Edition. Taylor & Francis, Inc., 1997.

Boal, Augusto and Adrian Jackson. *Games for Actors and Non-actors.* Second Edition. Taylor & Francis, Inc., 2002.

Book, Stephen. *Book on Acting.* Silman-James Press, 2001.

Brandes, Donna and Howard Phillips. *Gamesters' Handbook.* Thornes, Nelson, 1995.

Caltagirone, Dennis. *Theatre Arts: The Dynamics of Acting.* Fourth Edition. NTC Publishing Group, 1997.

Cassady, Marsh. *Acting Games.* Meriwether Publishing Ltd., 1993.

Caruso, Sandra and Susan Kosoff. *The Young Actor's Book of Improvisation.* Heinemann, 1998.

Diggles, Dan. *Improv for Actors.* Allworth Press, 2004.

Edelstein, Linda N. *The Writer's Guide to Character Traits.* F&W Publications, Inc., 2004.

Foreman, Kathleen and Clem Martini. *Something Like a Drug.* Red Deer Press, 1998.

Frager, Robert, ed. *Who Am I?* Penguin Group, 1994.

Hall, William and Paul Killam, ed. *The San Francisco Bay Area Theatresports Playbook, Edition 5.3.* Bay Area TheatreSports, 1998.

Halpern, Charna, Del Close, and Kim Howard Johnson. *Truth in Comedy.* Meriwether Publishing Ltd., 1994.

Hazenfield, Carol. *Acting on Impulse: The Art of Making Improv.* Coventry Creek Press, 2002.

Heimburg, Jason and Justin Heimburg. *The Official Movie Plot Generator.* Brothers Heimburg Publishing, Llp., 2004.

Horn, Delton T. *Comedy Improvisation.* Meriwether Publishing Ltd., 1991.

Izzo, Gary. *The Art of Play.* Heinemann, 1997.

Johnston, Chris. *House of Games.* Taylor & Francis, Inc., 1998.

Johnstone, Keith. *Impro.* Taylor & Francis, Inc., 1987.

Johnstone, Keith. *Impro for Storytellers.* Taylor & Francis, Inc., 1999.

Keirsey, David. *Please Understand Me II.* Prometheus Nemesis Book Company, Inc., 1998.

Koppett, Kat. *Training to Imagine: Practical Improvisational Theatre Techniques.* Stylus Publishing, LLC, 2001.

Kozluwaki, Robert. *The Art of Chicago Improv.* Heinemann, 2002.

Libera, Anne. *The Second City Almanac of Improvisation.* Northwestern University Press, 2004.

Lynn, Bill. *Improvisation for Actors and Writers.* Meriwether Publishing Ltd., 2004.

Neelands, Jonothan, et. al. *Structuring Drama Work.* Revised Edition. Cambridge University Press, 2000.

Novelly, Maria. *Theatre Games for Young Performers.* Meriwether Publishing Ltd., 1991.

O'Neill, Cecily, et. al. *Drama Guidelines.* Heinemann, 1977.

Peterson, Lenka and Dan O'Connor. *Kids Take the Stage.* Watson-Guptill Publications, Inc., 1997.

Pollak, Michael. *Musical Improv Comedy.* Masteryear Publishing, 2004.

Salas, Jo. *Improvising Real Life.* Revised Edition. Tusitala, 1993.

Seham, Amy E. *Whose Improv is it Anyway?* University Press of Mississippi, 2001.

Scher, Amy. *101 Ideas for Drama.* Heinemann, 1988.

Schanker, Harry. *The Stage and the School.* The McGraw-Hill Companies, 1997.

Sima, Judy and Kevin Cordi. *Raising Voices.* Libraries Unlimited, 2003.

Spolin, Viola. *Improvisation for the Theatre.* Third Edition. Northwestern University Press, 1999.

Spolin, Viola. *Theatre Games for Rehearsal.* Northwestern University Press, 1985.

Spolin, Viola. *Theatre Games for the Classroom.* Northwestern University Press, 1990.

Tarlington, Carole and Patrick Verriour. *Role Drama.* Heinemann, 1991.

Way, Brian. *Development Through Drama.* Prometheus Books, 1987.

About the Authors

Justine Jones
photo by Lee G. Weinland, III

Justine Jones and **Mary Ann Kelley** have collaborated on two drama and theatre curriculum guides for public schools in addition to *Improv Ideas: A Book of Games and Lists* and *Drama Games and Improvs: Games for the Classroom and Beyond* from Meriwether Publishing. They have also collaborated on numerous productions and drama festivals in their former home of Los Alamos, New Mexico.

Justine has taught improvisation and play production on the secondary level for thirty-four years. Her drama education studies have led her to England and Canada as well as several colleges in the U.S. Justine is also trained in psychodrama and drama therapy. Many of the ideas in this book are the result of suggestions from her students. All have been tested and refined in Justine's classrooms for over three decades and have been proven intellectually stimulating and creatively successful.

Justine now resides in London, England, where she continues her work in storytelling and improvisation. She is currently at work on *Mystery and Murder in the Middle School: A guide to writing and producing interactive murder mysteries with secondary school students*. She is furthering her studies at the London Centre for Psychodrama where she is also taking courses in improvisation, playback theatre, and sociodrama. She delights in a massive amount of London theatre.

Mary Ann has taught drama and directed kids in regular school settings and as enrichment for schools and recreation departments for over thirty years. Her recent focus has been the development of plays by and for young people through improvisation. She has directed and taught creative dramatics in multi-grade (grades 3-12) groups for over twenty years. She uses the games in *Improv Ideas* and the lessons in *Drama Games and Improvs* as creative prompts for original student-created plays as well as rehearsal tools for scripted plays. Mary Ann wrote the standards-based drama curriculum for fourth through sixth grades for Los Alamos, NM Public Schools.

Mary Ann lives in McIntosh, Florida. She directs children's plays — both scripted and kid-created; directs and techs with adults; attends as many theatrical events as possible; and

Mary Ann Kelley
photo by Lee G. Weinland, III

voraciously reads everything from plays and classics to "trashy crime fiction." She is now at work on *Creating Theatre in Twenty Hours*, a step-by-step guide designed for recreation leaders and teachers with too little time. *Creating Theatre in Twenty Hours* is a compilation of the techniques she used in fifteen years of teaching two-week summer school sessions in creative dramatics, each culminating in performances of original plays.

Order Form

Meriwether Publishing Ltd.
PO Box 7710
Colorado Springs CO 80933-7710
Phone: 800-937-5297   Fax: 719-594-9916
Website: www.meriwether.com

Please send me the following books:

_____ **Improv Ideas   #BK-B283** $24.95
by Justine Jones and Mary Ann Kelley
A book of games and lists

_____ **Drama Games and Improvs   #BK-B296** $22.95
by Justine Jones and Mary Ann Kelley
Games for the clasroom and beyond

_____ **Short & Sweet Skits for Student Actors   #BK-B312** $17.95
by Maggie Scriven
55 sketches for teens

_____ **Theatre Games for Young Performers #BK-B188** $17.95
by Maria C. Novelly
Improvisations and exercises for developing acting skills

_____ **Group Improvisation   #BK-B259** $16.95
by Peter Gwinn with additional material by Charna Halpern
The manual of ensemble improv games

_____ **275 Acting Games: Connected   #BK-B314** $19.95
by Gavin Levy
A comprehensive workbook of theatre games for developing acting skills

_____ **112 Acting Games   #BK-B277** $17.95
by Gavin Levy
A comprehensive workbook of theatre games

**These and other fine Meriwether Publishing books are available at your
local bookstore or direct from the publisher. Prices subject to change
without notice. Check our website or call for current prices.**

Name: _____ e-mail: _____

Organization name: _____

Address: _____

City: _____ State: _____

Zip: _____ Phone: _____

❑ **Check enclosed**
❑ **Visa / MasterCard / Discover / Am. Express #** _____

Signature: _____ *Expiration date:* _____ / _____ *CVV code:* _____
                 (required for credit card orders)

Colorado residents: Please add 3% sales tax.
Shipping: Include $3.95 for the first book and 75¢ for each additional book ordered.

❑ *Please send me a copy of your complete catalog of books and plays.*

About the *Improv Ideas* CD-ROM

The CD-ROM for *Improv Ideas* contains printable PDF files of every list in this book. The lists are available in two formats: Avery 5160 Labels and Print-and-Cut Strips.

To view the PDF files, you will need Adobe Reader. You can download Adobe Reader for free at www.adobe.com.